The Privilege of Preaching

A Book for Lay Preachers

Charles Henry Gay

Copyright

New minister at Bedford Street, Stroud, 1932

Dedications

In loving memory of Dad

(Sue & Chris Wensley - editors)

Original Dedication:

In memory of my father,

JAMES HENRY (HARRY) GAY,

who found great delight in many years' service as a Lay Preacher; and in tribute to the great host of Lay Preachers (many of whom have helped me personally in the churches where I have ministered) who gave their dedicated service to the Church of Jesus Christ.

Foreword

The Revd. Charles Henry Gay (1906-1975) was born and brought up in Treforest, South Wales. He began his ministry at Bedford Street Congregational church, Stroud in 1932.

He moved to Bushey Congregational church, Hertfordshire, in 1939, ministering there until 1947 when he received a call to Gloucester Street Congregational church, Weymouth (now, sadly, demolished).

Finally, in January 1962, he moved to New Trinity Congregational church, Canton, Cardiff. (This church became a United Reformed Church in 1972, and in 1995 it amalgamated with the Llandaff Road Baptist Chapel to form the Canton Uniting Chapel.) He remained at New Trinity until his death through ill health in 1975.

This book was started in the 1960s, the intention being to pass on his experience to lay preachers setting out on their ministry. In the early 1970s there was at last a completed version and, with the assistance of one of the editors, attempts were made for publication. Unfortunately, this did not happen prior to his passing, and the book has lain in a cupboard through the following decades.

On recently re-reading the original manuscript, it became clear that many quotations or illustrations had become outdated. However, in essence much of the material seemed relevant to the needs of ministers, lay preachers and students today.

What follows is an abridged version of the original manuscript. Biblical quotations have been changed from early versions (*Authorised Version* or *Revised Standard Version*) to the *New International Version* (NIV).

Perhaps the language belongs to a bygone age, but the character of the author shines through - a man of deep personal faith who dedicated his life to caring for his congregation. In addition, he worked hard as a hospital chaplain, a youth club leader and a pastoral visitor.

Revd. Gay was a passionate and inspired preacher. Examples of his sermons came to light more recently, and can be found in Part 3 of this book, together with a series of talks entitled *"Breakfast for the Mind"* for BBC Radio 4's *"Lift up your Hearts"*.

The books and authors he refers to here may possibly be unfamiliar to present-day readers, but these sermons have remained unabridged in order to preserve the original sense and spirit in which they were first delivered. Revd. Gay died in 1975 but, throughout this book, his words and thoughts live on.

It is only now, in 2023, when there are so many more opportunities for self-publishing, that this book can finally appear.

At Gloucester Street, Weymouth, 1958

Contents

Part 1   **Preparing the Preacher**   **1**

Chapter 1   Preaching Today   2
Chapter 2   Preaching changes lives   6
Chapter 3   The call to preach   11
Chapter 4   What shall I preach?   23
Chapter 5   The Preacher's Personality   35

Part 2   **Preparing the Sermon**   **45**

Chapter 1   Sowing sermon seeds   46
Chapter 2   Topics, Themes, Texts & Titles   54
Chapter 3   The Sermon Structure   65
Chapter 4   Introductions and Conclusions   73
Chapter 5   The necessity of illustrations   87
Chapter 6   Conclusion - The day of delivery   96

Part 3   **Meditations and Sermons**   **111**

1.   Radio 4: "Breakfast for the Mind"   112
2.   Address at a Young Peoples' Service   128
3.   Teach your children   137
4.   The Prayer Life of Jesus   145
5.   "A man reaps what he sows"   151
6.   "Yet ..."   158
7.   Faith founded on Facts   164
8.   Worrying? - Don't   171

Celebrating 40 years in the ministry, Cardiff, 1972

PART ONE :

PREPARING THE PREACHER

Chapter 1 - Preaching Today

No-one can really teach you how to preach. However, by listening to others, ministers and laymen, you will see that effective preachers have something in common. They are arresting, catching the interest of the congregation from the start, and holding it. They are logical, presenting their ideas in orderly sequence. They are simple and clear. They have personality, the truth coming through their humour, sincerity, enthusiasm, dedication. And they all give the impression of being used as channels through which God's truth flows to others.

The Gospel stands unchanged. The Truth remains the same yesterday, today, and forever. The message preached by Spurgeon, Wesley, Whitfield, Luther, Paul, is, in essence, the same message you will preach next Sunday. But while the basic message remains the same, you must present it against the background of contemporary situations and events. The Gospel must be re-interpreted to meet the needs, hopes, and fears, of these modern days.

Today there is a lack of interest in preaching and preachers, and the task itself is more difficult than it was in earlier times. A critical spirit is abroad. The accepted rules of Christian living and the fundamental doctrines of the Christian faith are not allowed to go unchallenged. But because of this atmosphere of indifference, disillusionment, and disbelief, the task of preaching becomes more important and glorious. This is why I have entitled this book *'The Privilege of Preaching'*. It is the greatest privilege to help in the adventurous, exciting, exhilarating task of preaching the Gospel.

Think back to the preachers of the early Church. The message they proclaimed helped them to cause trouble everywhere (Acts 17 v.6). "I am so eager to preach!" (Romans 1 v.15) cried Paul. The words tell of the thrill, the wonder, the exhilaration, the privilege of preaching.

The Purpose of Preaching

The purpose of preaching is to change lives, and to strengthen and nourish those who already believe. It is to spread the good news; to convince others; and to lead them to share the same peace and joy which we, as preachers, possess.

The purpose of preaching is to be found in its results. It is to present a challenge. This is what happened when John the Baptist preached. "The people asked him, saying, 'What should we do then?'" (Luke 3 v.10).

Peter won the same response. "When the people heard this, they were cut to the heart and said to Peter and the other apostles, 'Brothers, what shall we do?'" (Acts 2 v.37). So, a preacher should attempt to make God real to the congregation, to bring to them a sense of God's presence, and to interpret for them the will of God.

The Importance of Preaching

In 1949 Dr. Sangster said "Preaching is in the shadows." Such words are still true today as ministers turn to discussion groups, video clips, and house groups instead of preaching. There are those who say "We do not go to church to hear someone talk. We go to hold communion with God in praise and prayer." According to this view, prayer, praise, and the celebration of the sacraments are things that belong to God; preaching is merely human, coming from the mind of man.

This attitude is based upon a misconception of preaching. *If* a sermon is merely a literary essay or an elocutionary display; *if* the pulpit is no more than a substitute or a rival to the Sunday newspaper; *if* a man's sermon is just the formulation of a body of human ideals; *if* the pulpit is just another platform for the expression of personal opinions; *if* the preacher is just a religious commentator on current events; then indeed, the setting of worship apart from and above preaching would be justified. But preaching is none of these *ifs*. Preaching *is* worship. Praise, prayer and preaching belong to the same whole and cannot be separated.

Preaching was the foremost activity of the Apostles. It was through their preaching that the Church was brought into being. It was preaching that, in periods of flatness and failure, the Church was revived and restored. It is by preaching that the Church continues to be planted in modern times.

Preaching in the Early Church

Even a cursory reading of the New Testament leaves no doubt as to the place preaching held in the Early Church.

At the beginning of the ministry of John the Baptist are the words, "In those days John the Baptist came, *preaching* in the wilderness of Judea." (Matthew 3 v.1).

After His Baptism and the Temptations in the wilderness Jesus Himself began preaching. He took up the message from His fore-runner: "From that time on Jesus began to preach,

'Repent, for the kingdom of heaven has come near.'"
(Matthew 4 v.17).

The later life of Jesus is described in the words "Jesus
went through all the towns and villages, *teaching* in their
synagogues, *proclaiming* the good news of the kingdom ..."
(Matthew 9 v.35).

After the Ascension of their Master, the apostles took up
His mission. The last verse in Mark's Gospel reads: "Then the
disciples went out and *preached everywhere*, and the Lord
worked with them ..." (Mark 16 v.20).

There is no doubt as to the importance of preaching in the
mind of Paul. He was an apostle - one sent - an ambassador of
Jesus Christ - representing his King in a foreign country, and
making known the will of his King. Travelling from place to
place, preaching to small groups or to crowds, Paul established
churches, knowing full well, as he himself declared, that "Christ
did not send me to baptize, but to preach the gospel ..."
(1 Corinthians 1 v.17).

So the importance of preaching cannot be overestimated.
A preacher is God's ambassador, freely giving what he himself
has received from God. He can claim, humbly yet confidently,
to stand in the succession of prophets and apostles.

Chapter 2 : Preaching Changes Lives

As you preach, let the words of William Carey be in the forefront of your minds: "Attempt great things for God; expect great things from God."

God is in action through you. In your congregation there are people with difficulties, needs, problems, anxieties, fears …. If the preaching of the Gospel cannot help them, what can?

There is no reason why your preaching should not bring results. Sometimes dramatic results, completely changing lives. It can remove fear; give comfort to the sorrowing; hope to the depressed; restore strength and courage to those who are about to give up; and bring peace of heart to those anxious and worried by life's experiences.

A new message

D. L. Moody, founder of the Bible School in Northfield, U.S.A., gained a new conception of his Christian message through the preaching of another man. It was in Dublin that he met Harry Moorhouse, a converted pickpocket who had served time in prison before he was twenty-one years of age, but who had acquired a small reputation as a preacher. Moorhouse told Moody that he would like to come to Chicago and preach for him. Moody rather brushed him off, not seeing much in this young man whom he thought of as rather pestering him.

When he was back in America, Moody received a letter to say that Moorhouse had arrived in New York, and would preach in Chicago if Moody wished it. Once again, Moody tried to brush him off, replying, "If you come West, call on me." Then he put Moorhouse out of his mind.

But Moorhouse was not the sort of man who could be forgotten. He turned up in Chicago, and Moody simply had to give him the opportunity of preaching at his Mission. Moorhouse preached from the text "For God so loved the world that he gave his one and only Son ..." (John 3 v.16).

Moody was captivated, and humbled. He realised that his own message would have to be changed. Up till this time Moody had been preaching that God hated the sinner as well as the sin. Now this approach to preaching was in ruins. It was the love of God which must be the heart of his message. This, Harry Moorhouse had shown him in one sermon. From this time onward, Moody became the apostle of the love of God.

Look, look, look!

Charles Spurgeon's life was changed because he heard a lay preacher at a Primitive Methodist Church in Colchester. His conversion happened on a snowy day. The weather was so bad that it was felt inadvisable for him to go with his father from Colchester to Tollesbury where his father conducted services at the Independent Church. So he set out to attend a chapel locally, and found the Primitive Methodist Chapel in an obscure street.

Because of the inclement weather there were very few people in the congregation. So few indeed, that the lay preacher who was conducting the service wondered whether or not to preach his sermon. After some hesitation he announced his text, "Turn to me and be saved, all you ends of the earth; for I am God, and there is no other." (Isaiah 45 v.22).

"He set his eyes on me as if he knew all that was in my heart," says Spurgeon, "and then he said, 'Young man, you are in trouble. You will never get out of it until you look to Christ.' Then he lifted up his hands and cried, 'Look, look, look!'"

Like a secret suddenly revealed, the truth flashed upon the mind of Spurgeon. He had been waiting to do fifty things to find ease of mind and fellowship with God. Now he knew. All he had to do was look. It was as when the bronze serpent was lifted up by Moses, and all Israel had to do was look and be healed (Numbers 21 v.9).

In the evening he attended the Baptist Church at Colchester with his mother. Afterwards he talked long into the night with his father about what had happened during the day. "In the text, 'Look', I found salvation this morning; in the text 'accepted in the Beloved', I found peace and pardon tonight."

Several years after his conversion Mr. Spurgeon preached at the Primitive Methodist Chapel in Colchester. He took as his text the words which had changed his life. "That was the text I heard in this Chapel," he said, and, pointing to a seat under the gallery, he continued, "I was sitting in that pew when I was converted."

So to that single sermon, almost not preached, we owe the preaching of a man who built a college for preachers; who built a home for orphans; and who, through his sermons, transformed thousands of lives.

The decisive interjection

The story of Sir Wilfred Grenfell is well known. Faced with a choice of going to Oxford with his brother, or joining his father (a London hospital chaplain) to work in a hospital preparatory to becoming a doctor, he chose the latter.

It was in his second year, returning from an out-patient case at night, that he passed a tent where a Sankey and Moody mission was being held. He stepped inside to see what was going on.

Somebody was praying a long, tedious prayer, and he started to leave. Suddenly Moody called out, "While our brother is finishing his prayer, let us sing a hymn." This interjection made Grenfell change his mind and he stayed through the service.

When he left it was with this determination - either to make a real effort to do as Christ would do in his place as a doctor, or frankly, to abandon religion.

Moody's message had been a challenge. It brought him face to face with himself and with his religious profession. Later, he went to hear the brothers J. E. and T. C. Studd at a subsidiary meeting of the Moody campaign. As a result of their preaching he responded to their appeal and stood up as one who intended to follow Christ. The preaching of Moody and the Studd brothers made Wilfred Grenfell, *'Grenfell of Labrador'*.

Charles Hulbert (1778-1857) may not be so well known, but his whole life was one glorious chapter of changed lives. For example, during his ministry at Blackburn, he was forced to hold his services in the Palace Theatre because his Mission Hall was inadequate to receive all who wanted to attend. At the end of his first year, he received a letter from a woman who said that after hearing him preach for nearly a year she felt compelled to write and thank him for what he had done for her.

Through his preaching she had found strength to conquer her drinking habits, and to overcome her foolish way of living. Her home life was happier than she had ever known it. There were still anxieties, troubles and problems, but she was able to write that "This has been the happiest twelve months of my life."

What a tribute to the preaching which had caused such a change and brought such happiness.

Here then, are living examples of the purpose of preaching and the power of preaching. Never underestimate the task to which you are called. It is a great Gospel you have to preach. God uses preaching and preachers to change and transform lives.

Chapter 3 : The Call to Preach

God used Peter and God used Paul. Whether a man be Pharisee or fisherman, what is needed for a preacher is that he should feel the winds of God blowing through him. This is the crux of the matter. There is a divine urge which the preacher cannot disobey. Paul knew it. Every true preacher knows it. "Woe to me if I do not preach the gospel!" (1 Corinthians 9 v.16).

If you ask ministers or experienced lay preachers what it was that first drew them into the work of preaching, though their ostensible reasons may be multitudinous in their diversity, at the heart of the matter they will all agree on this - the call to preach.

Sometimes the call comes, as it were, against a man's will. Moses was prepared to do the whole bidding of God - except to speak for Him. Ezekiel shrank from the task. For years Chrysostom tried to evade it. Augustine turned in every direction before he plunged. Luther and John Knox begged to be excused.

Their lack of readiness to preach was not that they were unwilling to serve God in this way, but that they were conscious of their own inadequacy. All true preachers have felt this - a sense of unfitness, unworthiness. This constantly haunts a person, and, providing that it does not paralyse them, it adds to their effectiveness as a preacher. It throws them back upon God in utter dependence.

Dr. William Barclay tells of a party of tourists who were visiting Germany and were being shown into the room where Beethoven lived and worked. In one corner stood an old piano which was said to be the very instrument on which he had composed the famous "Moonlight Sonata". One of the tourists, an American girl, rushed to the piano and thumped out the first movement of the sonata. She turned to the group with an air of triumph. The guide remarked "You will be interested to know that we had Paderewski himself as a visitor last week."

"Really," said the girl, "I bet he did just what I did; sat down and played that sonata."

"No, Miss," said the guide. "Everybody begged him to do so, but he said, 'No, no. I am not worthy.'"

To know that the congregation in front of you has come for strengthening, inspiration and comfort; and to know that there are those who could, through preaching, meet their needs; and to be aware of your own insufficiency ... yes, the preacher has enough to keep him humble.

My own beginning

The first time I preached was at a little Baptist Church in South Wales. My father was a lay preacher and had an engagement at this church which was a few miles from home. Having undergone a serious operation he was, although home from hospital, unable to fulfil his engagement. All attempts to get a friend to take the appointment for him were in vain. I well remember running around to ask each one, but all his fellow preachers were themselves engaged.

Saturday evening arrived and the position was desperate. My father could not go himself, and could get no-one to go for him. It seemed as though he would have to 'let down' the church - a thing that had never happened before.

Why I did it, I do not know, but seeing his distress, I suggested, tentatively, that if he gave me one of his sermons I would go and read it for him. He accepted the suggestion with alacrity, and then I began to be more than a little sorry I had made it. I had never taken a service before.

The next morning came. I went to the Church, The sermon, which my father assured me would last twenty-five minutes, I read in ten. Although I added a few words of my own when I came to the end of the sermon, to spin it out, the whole service was over in forty minutes.

After the service I was thanked by one of the deacons with the encouraging words: "Well, well, boy; you were better than nobody."

After my father had fully recovered, I often went with him on his preaching appointments, taking part in the service, giving the children's addresses, and occasionally preaching the sermons - my own, by now!

With this I was quite content, until, one Sunday morning, at a local Methodist Church, when my father made his usual request that I should take part in the service and preach the sermon, the steward in charge refused to let me preach because I was not a qualified preacher.

He was probably well within his rights in acting so, and undoubtedly he had the welfare of the church at heart, but I was bitterly disappointed at the time. After consultation with my parents, it was decided that, if I could not preach without being qualified, then I would qualify. By now the desire to preach was strong within me.

I consulted my minister, Dr. Rees Griffiths, and arrangements were made for him to train me for the Local Preachers' examination (as it was then called). I have not sat for that examination yet. It was while I was studying with Dr. Rees Griffiths that he made the suggestion that I should sit for the entrance examination at New College, London, and train for the ministry. The result of that startling suggestion does not belong to this book. I have said enough to show how I started.

Destiny comes sideways

The call to preach comes in different ways, but you can depend upon it that if God means you to preach He will let you know. Here are a few examples.

Moses, roused by the suffering of his people, tried to help them. He failed (Exodus 2). Years afterwards, when all thoughts of serving his people must have passed from his mind (or if the thought had not passed, the opportunity obviously had) the challenge came (Exodus, 3&4).

Paul, eager to go to Bithynia, found himself up against a blank wall. Surely the opportunity to preach the Gospel was there, but everything stood in his way: "… they tried to enter Bithynia, but the Spirit of Jesus would not allow them to." (Acts 16 v.7). It was after this experience that the call came: "Come over to Macedonia and help us." (Acts 16 v.9). Destiny comes sideways.

Isaiah's call came out of extremity and personal tragedy. Uzziah, the king upon whom he depended for his future prosperity and advancement, had died. Anxious, fearful and with a heavy heart, Isaiah entered the temple. There the call came. His earthly king was dead; now he saw another King - the King Immortal. He saw a vision. God spoke. He was faced with a challenge.

"Whom shall I send? And who will go for us?"

There was no withstanding this challenge.

"And I said, 'Here am I. Send me!'"

"He said, 'Go and tell this people: ...'". (Isaiah 6 vv.8,9).

Jeremiah was one who shrank from the task of preaching. His own statement makes this abundantly clear. When the call came, doubts and fears made him weak and trembling. "'Alas, Sovereign Lord,' I said, 'I do not know how to speak; I am too young.'" (Jeremiah 1 v.6). Yet, in spite of his fears, the conviction is there: "The word of the Lord came to me." (Jeremiah 1 v.4).

How it came we are not able to tell. Did it come from pondering over the moral and spiritual state of his nation? Was it that inner voice which is nothing strange to a man in fellowship with God? The conviction grew that from the beginning God had marked him out to preach His word. In spite of his fears he would have to go where God sent him, and speak what God commanded. The sense of compulsion is clear.

Amos was another whose call came through a sense of compulsion - the compulsion of circumstances. A shepherd and a vine-dresser in Tekoa in the Southern Kingdom, he sold his produce in the Northern Kingdom of Israel.

If ever there was an affluent society it was to be found in this Northern Kingdom. But underneath all the prosperity and apparent well-being there were evils which shocked this simple shepherd. The luxury and selfishness of the rich; the oppression of the poor; the bribery and corruption rampant in high places; left him dazed. Above everything else his soul was shaken by the hollowness and shallowness of their religion.

At last he could stand it no longer. He must speak out. He was only a simple shepherd, but he could not keep silent while such things existed.

"The lion has roared - who will not fear? The Sovereign Lord has spoken - who can but prophesy?" (Amos 3 v.8).

At last the crisis came. Amos takes a bold step. He goes to Bethel, to the king's sanctuary and the royal house. There he flings down the gauntlet, denouncing their evils and flinging his warnings in their teeth.

"I was no prophet, neither was I a prophet's son, ..." replied Amos, "But the Lord took me from tending the flock and said to me, 'Go, prophesy to my people Israel.' Now then, hear the word of the Lord." (Amos 7 vv.14-16).

What a dramatic scene. The lonely shepherd against the might of the king, his nobles, his priests, and the powers of organised religion. Here was a man who was shocked into preaching by the evils of society.

The call of the preacher, and the vision of God which sometimes accompanies the call, are two sides of the same experience. With Isaiah, the call sprang out of a vision. With Jeremiah the call came first and was later supplemented by experiences and visions. In the case of Amos there was no outward vision, only a growing conviction that things were wrong, and that God was calling him to say so!

So God leads men to preach His Word. The need of the times; the sense of compulsion; a way opening up; an opportunity given; an inward desire; a challenge we cannot ignore; in all these ways God calls men to preach.

An unexpected challenge

A preacher's first attempt at preaching is often made under peculiar and unexpected circumstances. It was so with Spurgeon. A friend was going to take a service at a little village a few miles from Cambridge, and Spurgeon was asked to go with him for company. On the way to the village church Spurgeon turned to his friend and expressed his good wishes saying, "I trust God will bless your labours tonight." His friend looked at him blankly. "I'm not taking the service," he said. "I've never preached in my life."

It transpired that someone had asked him to accompany Spurgeon, and he was under the impression that it was Spurgeon who was to take the service.

Two young men, walking together to a village church, neither of them ever having preached, and each expecting the other to conduct the service!

Arriving at the church, with his friend absolutely refusing to preach, Spurgeon, in the face of the assembled congregation, felt he must make some attempt at conducting the service.

His text was: "Now to you who believe, this stone is precious." (1 Peter 2 v.7). He was sixteen years old.

That happened in 1850. From that small beginning came thirty-seven volumes of sermons, a host of books, a multitude of booklets and tracts, all of which had a world-wide circulation.

In distant parts of the earth, where men were living in scattered communities, families would gather together for worship. For the central point of the service someone would read one of Spurgeon's sermons.

But much was to happen before the famous minister of the Metropolitan Tabernacle gained his world-wide fame. After his first sermon, Spurgeon preached at many of the villages around Cambridge, and eventually became lay pastor of the little church at Waterbeach.

It was then suggested, even urged by his father and many friends, that he should seek entrance to Regent's Park College to be better prepared for the ministry.

He felt the force of these arguments, and arrangements were made for him to meet Dr. Angus, the Principal of the college. They were to meet at the house of Mr. Macmillan, the publisher.

Arriving at the house, Spurgeon was shown into a room and asked to wait, as Dr. Angus had not arrived. He waited ... and waited ... and waited. Two hours passed, and at last he plucked up courage and rang the bell to find out the reason for the delay. The explanation was simple, yet exasperating. The servant had forgotten all about him! When Dr. Angus arrived he was shown into another room. After a period of waiting, he felt he was too busy to waste time on a young man who was so tardy in keeping appointments, so he left.

Thoroughly disappointed, Spurgeon decided to write to the college to make an application for admission. The same afternoon, however, as he walked over Midsummer Common on his way to a preaching engagement at Chesterton, he was startled by a loud voice which said, "Should you then seek great things for yourself? Do not seek them." (Jeremiah 45 v.5).

Whatever explanation modern psychologists may give to this incident, it made a difference to Spurgeon. He himself freely admitted that "it may have been a singular illusion", but the impression it made on him was most vivid. He renounced any idea of a college course, and devoted himself to the little village congregation at Waterbeach.

His father's message

"Prepare your own sermons. Just tell the people that Jesus Christ can change lives. Love, Dad."

That was the disappointing message which came to Norman Vincent Peale (later the well-known minister of Marble Collegiate Church, New York) when he was a student.

The church at Walpole, Massachusetts needed someone for a Sunday service in a few weeks' time. Norman Peale volunteered to go, and for two full weeks worked feverishly on his sermon. It was to be his first attempt at preaching. He wanted everything to go well.

He chose a text he had often heard his father preach from: "I have come that they may have life, and have it to the full." (John 10 v.10). He wrote and re-wrote that sermon. He prepared it in at least seven different versions. Not one of them satisfied him.

On the Monday before the dreaded Sunday he wrote in panic to his father: "I wish you would send me your notes or any written copy you have of the sermon I have heard you preach so often from this text. Please send anything you have AT ONCE." The reply we have seen.

The Sunday came. He arrived at the church early and was shown into a room with an old red couch and a table strewn with hymn books and church announcements. There he was left to wait while the church secretary went off to see to his duties.

He paced up and down the room trying to fix his sermon in his mind. He was growing more and more terror-stricken every moment. Through the window he could see the congregation beginning to gather. He saw an elderly man, tall and stately, come towards the church. At the sight of him Norman Peale's assurance died away.

"What have you got to say that could possibly mean anything to a man like that? Who are you to be telling him how to conduct his life?" A jeering voice seemed to be asking these questions, and he had no answer.

Feeling utterly inadequate he fell upon his knees and prayed with an urgency he had never felt before: "Help me, Lord. Help me to say something that will help them."

The church secretary came to fetch him. The panic had gone. He felt a great calmness of mind and heart. His first sermon lasted only twelve minutes. He forgot all about his prepared sermon. He simply tried to tell the congregation what Christ had done for him, and could do for them, if they would let Him.

Although in later years he preached much longer sermons, his theme was always the same. He never forgot his father's message: "Just tell the people that Jesus Christ can change lives."

His mother's prayers

Dr. Leslie Weatherhead was one of those who, as a child, conducted services in his home. He was greatly encouraged by his mother who always wanted him to be a minister. She confided to him that she had constantly prayed for this, even before he was born.

As a youth he saw Jesus as a hero figure. Here was someone who, in His life, exemplified all the finest qualities that compel admiration and allegiance. Hence, there came to him the burning desire to tell others what Jesus meant to him.

His first sermon was preached at Houghton-on-the-Hill, a little village in Leicestershire. It was only a small congregation, but in his extreme nervousness, he unconsciously tore the cord round the cushion of the pulpit desk.

Weatherhead's text for his first sermon was: "Come to me, all you who are weary and burdened, and I will give you rest." (Matthew 11 v.28). He came away from that service more deeply convinced than ever that God was calling him to preach.

For his second sermon, preached shortly afterwards, he took as his text: "The apostles left the Sanhedrin, rejoicing because they had been counted worthy of suffering disgrace for the Name." (Acts 5 v.41). Thus, his first sermon was the expression of the poetic side of his nature. The second sermon illustrated what had always appealed strongly to him - religion as adventure.

Such are the ways in which the 'call' comes. Such are the occasions on which first sermons have been preached. Different ways, different circumstances, but in them you may see a reflection of your own call to preach. On the other hand, your experience may be entirely different. For there is no set way for the 'call' or the 'occasion'. When the 'call' comes, however it comes - you will know!

Chapter 4 : What shall I Preach?

The content of our preaching depends upon our purpose. What you preach is determined by what you hope to achieve. For example, your aim may be one of the following:-

1) Vindicate the Christian faith and establish its relevance to modern life.

2) Deepen the congregation's understanding of God, and awaken or confirm faith.

3) Teach the holy love of God to elicit a response of adoration.

4) Help men re-discover their moral and social obligations to one another in Christian brotherhood.

5) Interpret passages from the Bible.

Let us look at some of these purposes in more detail.

Apologetic

First, the so-called apologetic type of preaching - preaching which is an explanation, a defence, and a vindication of the Gospel.

The Apostles used this type of preaching when they appealed to the Jewish Scriptures to vindicate the preaching of the Christian faith.

Read again Peter's sermon at Pentecost. See how he appeals to the prophet Joel, and to David when speaking of the death and resurrection of Jesus, and the outpouring of the spirit of God. These events were the fulfilment of prophecy.

Paul similarly argues from the Jewish Scriptures proclaiming that "Christ died for our sins according to the

Scriptures; and that he was buried, and that he rose again the third day according to the Scriptures. (1 Corinthians 15 vv.3-4).

C. S. Lewis in his books *'Mere Christianity'*, *'The Problem of Pain'* and *'The Screwtape Letters'* met the doubts and arguments of genuine enquirers and sophisticated sceptics by presenting a reasonable, credible, defensible interpretation of the Christian Gospel.

Although this is not the type of preaching to be used every Sunday, as preachers you will know at first hand the arguments of the humanists, the caricatures of Christianity, the misunderstandings of what the Church really believes, which you find among those whom you meet in your daily work. There are those in your congregations who have also to meet taunts, misunderstandings, objections, arguments, in their offices, shops and factories. To these, the Apologetic type of preaching can be of great service.

Devotional

Devotional preaching is that which deals with the secrets of the inner life and the deepening of our fellowship with God.

There is a hunger in the heart of men for God. "Oh, that you would rend the heavens and come down." (Isaiah 64 v.1). "If only I knew where to find him." (Job 23 v.3). "As the deer pants for streams of water, so my soul pants for you, my God. My soul thirsts for God, for the living God." (Psalm 42 vv.1-2). "Lord, show us the Father and that will be enough for us." (John 14 v.8). "Thou hast made us for Thyself, and our hearts are restless till they find their rest in Thee." (Augustine).

It is to this need that devotional preaching speaks. There is a touch of mysticism in it. Worship, prayer, meditation, holiness of life, the aspirations of the heart, deepened communion with God - these are the realms in which you move when you preach a devotional sermon.

Some preachers are afraid that devotional preaching will be impractical and airy-fairy, but this is not necessarily the case. Dr. Sangster once linked together devotional and ethical preaching. He said "Once, I preached on the 'Sense of the Presence of God' from the text "God did this so that they would seek him and perhaps reach out for him and find him, though he is not far from any one of us. 'For in him we live and move and have our being.'" (Acts 17 v.28). I emphasised that a sense of God's presence was an essential part of our faith. This theme ran like a golden thread through the Bible. It culminated in the Incarnation. Here the Word became flesh. He who came was called Emmanuel - God with us. My application of the text was extremely practical. If God is so near, we have to take a greater care in our living (ethical) and must have a greater zeal in our service to our fellows (social)."

There is a need for devotional preaching, for it leads to holiness of life, which leads to service and sacrifice.

Doctrinal

Doctrinal preaching is the setting forth in an orderly way the beliefs of the Church. Doctrine is the explanation of a spiritual fact.

We ask questions as to the 'why' and 'how' of our beliefs, and the answer to our questions are statements which become a doctrine or teaching of the Church. It is important in your preaching to take such questions as "What is Salvation?"; "Is there an after-life?"; "Is sin our fault?"; "How can I find God?"; "Does God care?" and try to answer them in clear, simple language. However cold and detached from life doctrines and dogmas may seem, they were developed to express the profound convictions of believing Christians. This is preaching through which a distracted world can hear the certainties of the Christian faith.

Ethical and moral

The outcome of belief is character. The goodness of God leads us to repentance, and repentance leads to holiness of life.

Ethical and moral preaching was the preaching of the prophets. Look at Nathan's condemnation of David's moral lapse when he had Uriah killed in battle in order to possess himself of Bathsheba (2 Samuel 12 vv.1-15).

See also how Elisha condemned Ahab for the way in which he gained possession of Naboth's vineyard.
(1 Kings 21 v.19).

This type of preaching was the key-note of the eighth century prophets. We have already noted how the soul of Amos was shocked at the luxury, selfishness, oppression, bribery and corruption which characterised the affluent society of the Northern Kingdom. "Away with the noise of your songs! I will not listen to the music of your harps. But let justice roll on like a river, righteousness like a never-failing stream!" (Amos 5 vv.23-24). The people tried to cover up their wickedness with the cloak of outward religion.

Equally scathing in his condemnation is the prophet Micah. "With what shall I come before the Lord? … Will the Lord be pleased with thousands of rams, with ten thousand rivers of olive oil?   Shall I offer my firstborn for my transgression? … He has shown you, O mortal, what is good. And what does the Lord require of you?   To act justly and to love mercy and to walk humbly with your God." (Micah 6 vv.6-8).

Here is ethical preaching at its best.   Not that these prophets belittled religious observances. What they emphasised was that ritual was of little use without righteousness.   Feasts, sacrifices, ceremonials, must go hand in hand with holiness of life.

Similarly, in the New Testament we are aware that true worship must issue in moral obedience to the will of God.

"By their fruit you will recognize them." said Jesus. (Matthew 7 v.16).

In the Sermon on the Mount Jesus deepens and intensifies the ethical preaching of the Old Testament. He places the moral quality of an action in the thought - the intention - which precedes the deed.   "You have heard that it was said to the people long ago … But I tell you … (Matthew 5 vv.21,22). Motive, intention, the inwardness of the action should be our chief concern.   Behind the murder is the anger and hatred; behind the adultery is the impure desire.

We need to hold up before our listeners high ethical ideals and moral standards, but ethical preaching must be based upon, and spring from the Gospel and communion with Christ.

Evangelistic

Evangelistic preaching sets out to win a person's total commitment to Christ.

The great key word of evangelistic preaching is *repentance*. This was the message of John the Baptist, and this was the message of Jesus Himself.

"Repent, for the kingdom of heaven has come near." (Matthew 3 v.2).

For a person to be brought to repentance there must be consciousness of sin. Rebellion against the law is crime; rebellion against morality is vice; rebellion against God is sin.

Repentance is not merely sorrow for sin, otherwise it would be indistinguishable from remorse. Repentance includes constructive action. It contains a willingness to turn round and begin again. Peter, after his denial of Jesus wept bitterly, and then devoted his life to the Master he had denied.

The aim of evangelistic preaching is to arouse a conviction of sin; a recognition of the need for forgiveness; a true repentance; and the acceptance of Christ by faith.

This is what Paul was doing when he and his helpers turned the world upside down. (Acts 17 v.6). It was this preaching which led to a revival under the Wesleys and Whitfield, and gave birth to the Salvation Army. We hear it again in Sankey, Moody, and Billy Graham.

In spite of our inventive genius and scientific progress, we are no longer certain of our self-sufficiency, and seem to have no answer for the uncertainty and restlessness of life. The world is full of broken hearts, broken lives, sorrow, suffering and sin. We still need the message of the Cross. The purpose of its love, sacrifice, and suffering can still bring us to a sense of our sinfulness; still give us the assurance of forgiveness; and still inspire us with a devotion to Christ.

Expository (textual)

Here, the preacher expounds, explains, interprets, sets forth clearly the meaning of a text or passage of Scripture.

Whole books of the Bible can be treated in this way. Jonah for example. Here is a book written to protest against the narrow exclusiveness and intolerance of the Jews. The story is familiar. God commanded Jonah to go to Nineveh and pronounce her doom and destruction. The prophet refused to go. He suspects that if, as a result of his message, Nineveh repents, God will pardon and forgive. He cannot bear the thought of a heathen people receiving the forgiveness of God. So he runs away - or tries to! Eventually, after trying in vain to escape his responsibility, he reaches Nineveh, and the city's doom is pronounced.

What he was afraid would happen, did happen! Nineveh repented. God forgave. Jonah was furious. What was the good of being a prophet if your predictions were unfulfilled?

He had to learn, as the nation had to learn, that the everlasting mercy is … everlasting and universal! Here is a book teaching tolerance and tenderness. The relevance of such teaching for today is obvious.

Expounding a chapter or Biblical passage is another method of expository preaching. Acts chapter 10 teaches a similar lesson as the book of Jonah. Two men had visions.

Cornelius, a Gentile; and Peter, a Jew. The chapter describes their visions, tells of their meeting, and relates the result of their encounter. Tradition was vanquished. New truth was born. Prejudice defeated, and a new step taken in the march toward human brotherhood.

"Then Peter began to speak: 'I now realize how true it is that God does not show favouritism but accepts from every nation the one who fears him and does what is right.'"
(Acts 10 vv.34,35).

Yet another way is to take a Biblical character and trace the references of this character through the Bible until you are able to present a real human personality from whose virtues and failings we may all be helped to live.

Take Demas, for instance. There are just three references to him in the New Testament. But what a story they tell, and what a warning they issue.

Demas, "my fellow worker". That is how Paul describes him to Philemon (v.24). One of the eager company of those who were spreading the faith. A young fellow responding to the responsibility involved in the privilege of belonging to the Christian community.

"Demas". Just the name and nothing else when Paul is writing to the Colossians (Colossians 4 v.14). Paul finishes his letter with greetings from those who are with him. Many names are mentioned. Paul has something to say about each of them ... except Demas.

The very fact that Tychicus, Onesimus, and the rest are described as a faithful worker, and fellow servant, or a dear and faithful brother, makes us more conscious that Demas is no more called a fellow worker. Still present, but ceasing to serve?

The last reference to Demas is in Paul's second letter to Timothy. Paul is coming to the end of his life. There is a touch of loneliness about this letter to Timothy. He longs for companionship. "Do your best to come to me quickly ... Get Mark and bring him with you." The reason? "Demas, because he loved this world, has deserted me and has gone to Thessalonica." (2 Timothy 4 vv.9-11).

It has happened. Demas has gone. Did he cease to serve because he could not stand the strain? Or did his enthusiasm begin to fade? What a contrast to the life of the man he deserted. What about a sermon on the "Perils of Renounced Service" based on this story of Demas?

Again, one can take a single verse, brood over it, ascertain its essential meaning, discover the truth it enshrines, the challenge it presents, its implications for present day life, and expound these things.

A most interesting way of exposition is to take a single word representing some great Biblical theme: Grace; Faith; Atonement; Salvation; or Covenant, for instance, and to trace its meaning in the Old and New Testaments.

There are rich rewards for a preacher who, by such expository methods, can make the Bible come alive for the congregation.

Social

Social … society … living together with our fellows. This is life's big problem. It is the inability to live together which is the cause of broken homes, broken relationships in industry, wars and rumours of wars among the nations. Can the preacher speak to these conditions?

The Lord's Prayer begins: "Our Father". We have emphasised the word "Father", but tended to forget the word "Our". These opening words speak not only of the Fatherhood of God, but of the brotherhood of man. If God is Father, then men are brothers.

Look again at the story of Cain and Abel. "The Lord asked Cain, 'Where is your brother Abel?'" (Genesis 4 v.9). In the parable of the Prodigal Son the father said: "But we had to celebrate and be glad, because this brother of yours …".
(Luke 15 v.32).

Here is the social nature of religion. Cain answers God's question thus: "Am I supposed to take care of my brother?" The answer of both Testaments is "I am my brother's brother."

There are two aspects of the social Gospel. The first, as we have already seen, deals with human relationships. The second deals with the social evils which tend to destroy those relationships. Both aspects are included in this type of preaching.

We have already seen how the prophets stressed the ethical note in their preaching; but the prophets were not only moralists. They were social reformers. This was their proclamation: religious observances are useless unless they lead to ethical and moral living, and personal morality is fruitless unless it leads to social reformation.

The Christian idea as taught and lived by Jesus is summed up in the word 'love' He commended the lawyer's summary of the law - "'Love the Lord your God with all your heart and with all your soul and with all your strength and with all your mind'; and 'Love your neighbour as yourself.'" "You have answered correctly," Jesus replied (Luke 10 vv.27-28). This is the social Gospel. Love to God issuing in love to men.

Answering the lawyer's question, "And who is my neighbour?" Jesus told the matchless story of the Good Samaritan. This is the social Gospel. This explains what love means. Love means *sympathy*. "He took pity on him." (Luke 10 vv.30-35). Here was a sympathy which took precedence over nationalism. Not now, "Jews have no dealings with Samaritans" but "Here is a man who needs help, and I am a man who can give it." Humanity was greater than nationalism. From his heart there welled a sympathy which prompted the next practical application of love - *service*.

"He went over to him, poured oil and wine on his wounds and bandaged them." Here is something practical. He met his needs. This is the teaching of Jesus. Wherever there is need, and wherever we have the means to help, there we are to prove ourselves the good neighbour.

We pass from service to *sacrifice*. "He took out two denarii." Love is costly.

The social Gospel then, in both aspects, must be preached. The working out of social relationships, and the struggle against social evils through the power of love revealed through sympathy, service and sacrifice.

Yet you must be careful not to over-do this kind of preaching. Racial discrimination, and the plight of developing nations are problems that must be brought before modern congregations. The plight of the traveller in the story of the Good Samaritan is not merely a personal one, but an international one. But in dealing with the problems of the world the preacher must not ignore the problems of the individual. There must be some word for the sorrowing, the lonely, the tempted, and the weary. Society and individuals act and re-act upon one another. That is why the preacher must have a message for the individual heart, and for the heart of society.

I offered them Christ

To bring bread to the hungry, friendship to the lonely, comfort to the suffering, hope to the despairing, Christ's saving grace to the sinful ... that is the preacher's task. Whatever your sermons be in emphasis - apologetic, doctrinal, devotional, evangelistic, expository, social, your task is not simply to tell your congregation something, but to offer them Christ. This is your privilege and your joy.

Chapter 5 : The Preacher's Personality

(1) Be yourself

(a) It's you God wants

Preachers must be themselves so that the truth might come through their own personality. John was John; Peter was Peter; Paul was Paul. Each had the same truth to declare. Paul did not try to become Peter; neither did Peter try to become John. Liquid poured into a bottle is the same liquid whatever the shape of the bottle. Similarly, the message takes the shape of the personality of the preacher without disturbing its essence. The same truth comes through differing personalities.

"There was a man sent from God whose name was John." (John 1 v.6). He was John the Baptist. But there were other men sent from God whose names were John ... John Wesley, John Calvin, John Williams, John Smith, and many many other Johns - besides those whose names were Peter, or George, or Charles, or William etc .... What's your name?

All these were differing personalities declaring the truth in their own individual ways. So ... be yourself. Preaching demands of everyone the dedication of their own personality. You may not have great intellectual capacity, or fiery eloquence, or the quality of great persuasion, but you are you, with your own qualities, talents and personality. When God called you to preach He called you because you are you, not a copy of someone else. It's you God wants.

(b) A personal message

If you are to be yourselves, then your message must be personal. It is interesting to take note of the way in which Paul describes the Gospel. Many times he calls it "The Gospel of God". Often he calls it "The Gospel of His Son". Mostly he calls it "The Gospel of Christ". But at least twice (Hebrews 4 vv.2,6) he calls it "the Good News I proclaimed."

What does Paul mean by the "Good News"? Some verses in his second letter to the Corinthians might help to elucidate this. He writes, "All this is from God, ..." that is, all things connected with the regeneration of mankind. God is the source and origin of the new, as well as of the old creation. Having asserted this, Paul goes a step further and declares the historical fact through which the Divine power and love are manifested: "... who reconciled us to himself through Christ." (2 Corinthians 5 v.18).

Here is the essence of the Gospel. Jesus lived and taught and healed; was crucified, and rose from the dead. God was in Jesus. The redemptive purpose of God was revealed in Christ.

But the comprehensive scheme of God's grace was not yet complete. The redeeming mercy must be proclaimed to all. The Gospel must be preached. Therefore, "God was reconciling the world to himself in Christ, not counting people's sins against them. And he has committed to us the message of reconciliation." (2 Corinthians 5 v.19).

This was Paul's message - to implore men in the name of Christ to be reconciled to God.

You must preach your own message. You do not say something because you happen to be in the pulpit. You go into the pulpit because you have something to say, and that 'something' is the message you have received from God. You have received it through study, prayer, and meditation. God's truth is to be delivered through your own personality. This is your Gospel.

(c) A personal faith

If you are to have a personal message, then your faith must be your own faith. To you, as to everybody, religion first came second-hand. Through parents, Sunday School teachers, ministers, you were taught what they believed, and led to share, in greater or lesser degree, their experience of God. But those experiences, for you, were second-hand.

The trouble with a great many Christian people is that they have not progressed beyond this stage. They are trying to live their religious lives on the experiences of others. No wonder their religion is unsatisfying.

For a preacher to be in this position is tragic. If you are to preach to others, you must have a faith to proclaim. And it must be your faith. It must be a faith born of your experience of God through Christ. The study of religion is one thing; religious experience is another. You must possess in your own soul the faith and experience you offer to your fellows.

(2) Feed yourself

(a) Know your Bible

A preacher needs to probe deeply until he understands what the Biblical texts meant when they were first written or spoken. The Bible has its own message. We must say what it says, and not try to make it say what we would like it to say. The preacher must believe the Bible contains the eternal Gospel so relevant to human needs. It is confidence in the Bible which gives the preacher confidence in preaching. The Bible contains the eternal Gospel so relevant to human needs. With an open heart and mind; long, patient, reverent meditation and study; the preacher imbibes, receives, understands, and then creates the message.

Many famous preachers made a habit of reading the Bible in the original languages. Lay preachers may not be able to read Greek or Hebrew themselves, but they should take advantage of those who have used their scholarship in preparing translations to help them. *The New English Bible, The Living Bible*; the translations of J.B.Phillips; *The Good News Bible*; *New International Version* and *The Message* are among those which can be of the utmost value to the lay preacher. Compare these versions with one another, together with the Authorised, Revised, and Revised Standard versions, to gain a deeper understanding of the Bible. In addition be familiar with commentaries.

The writers in the Bible had understood some eternal truths. These they had to express in the language and ideas of their own day. Truth does not change. Ways of interpreting the truth do. Language alters and words change their meaning. Ancient truths must be expressed in modern words. Today is not yesterday. Preachers must be open-minded.

It is the preacher's task to interpret the Bible to those listening; to make the transition from ancient to modern times; and to show the congregation how these eternal truths are relevant to them. But a word of warning - as preachers we must be living daily with the Bible, but not merely to find texts and themes, but for our own spiritual nourishment. We go to the Bible to discover what God wants to say to us, as well as to find out what He wants us to say to others.

(b) Widen your interests by reading or surfing

It is good for a preacher to be aware of the problems, perplexities, longings, struggles and trials taking place in the world. News articles, comments and viewpoints are easily accessible on the web, and deal with the same item of news from different points of view. They can be a profitable source of ideas and illustrations, and offer an opportunity for preachers to think things out for themselves.

To the history of the world and of our own country must be added Church history. A local library should be able to provide volumes on the history of the Church in general, and the history of a particular denomination.

Biographical books, particularly biographies of preachers, lawyers, writers and missionaries give ample evidence of folk facing and overcoming difficulties of every kind. Many illustrations can be garnered from reading about their lives, and lessons learnt from their experiences.

Books about psychology help to give a glimmering of what makes people 'tick' - their moods and motives. In addition, scientific journals reveal what a truly amazing universe we inhabit. Scientific progress cannot be neglected, and need not be in opposition to religious belief. An amazing universe needs an amazing God as its creator.

Finally, books on theology - the science which deals with the relationship between God and His creation - are essential to help you first understand for yourself, and then preach to others (for example) the mysteries of the Incarnation, the Atonement, or the work of the Holy Spirit.

Thus, through reading biography; theology; psychology; science; as well as poetry and drama, you may be fed, and become more aware of the world in which you live.

(c) Kneel to conquer

I once preached a sermon on "The Prayer Life of Jesus", taking as my text "But Jesus often withdrew to lonely places and prayed." (Luke 5 v.16). *[See the fourth sermon in Part 3, p.145. - Ed.]*

In the sermon I dealt with six occasions on which Jesus prayed.

(1) Very early in the morning (Mark 1 v.35).

(2) At the end of the day (Mark 6 v.46).

(3) Before calling his disciples and choosing the twelve (Luke. 6 vv. 12-13).

(4) After the return of the seventy (Luke 10 v. 21).

(5) On the mountain of Transfiguration (Luke 9 v.28).

(6) In the Garden of Gethsemane (Luke 22 v.41).

Morning and evening; before and after a venture; in joy and in sorrow; Jesus prayed.

There is a need of prayer for every preacher who would preach to others. Lay preachers may find this difficult. Apart from their daily work, there are so many other demands upon their time. But time must be found for thought, meditation and prayer. Occasionally a sermon does not seem to inspire. Why did it fail despite all the preparation? Ask yourself: "Was it because I was so busy preparing my sermon that I omitted to prepare myself?" We must kneel to conquer.

(3) Give yourself

(a) Put in your hand

These words were spoken by Lawrence of Arabia. When one of Lawrence's Arab followers had performed some special service, he rewarded him by opening a bag of sovereigns, and saying to him, "Put in your hand."

This was thought to be the very height of splendour. One can easily imagine how plunging one's hand into a sack of gold, and helping oneself, could be much more thrilling than the careful counting out of a few hundred pounds.

Is this how you give to God? If you are to be truly His servant it is not enough to 'be yourself' and 'feed yourself'. You must 'give yourself'. Not cautiously measuring out your energy, effort and service; but, like Mary, with the alabaster box of ointment, pouring out yourself extravagantly in God's service. The preacher must give themselves completely into the hands of their Lord.

(b) Take my life

The opening lines of Frances Ridley Havergal's hymn,

Take my life and let it be
Consecrated, Lord, to thee

should be the preacher's Golden Text and constant prayer. First, because unless there is this self-giving, the preacher will find a lack of power and assurance in preaching. But also because we often preach far better sermons with our lives than with our lips. In any case, a sermon preached with the lips must be confirmed by the life.

Heed the words of St. Francis of Assisi: "Unless you preach everywhere you go, it is of no use to go anywhere to preach." The preacher's life is the final justification of his or her calling.

These then are the three essentials in the preparation of a preacher: be yourself; feed yourself; give yourself.

Bushey Congregational Church, Hertfordshire

PART TWO :

PREPARING THE SERMON

Chapter 1 : Sowing Sermon Seeds

No water from an empty well

To write a sermon you need resources - resources you have been storing up for years. As preachers you will be continually giving out, so there must be a replenishing of the store. If you are to avoid a sense of strain and stress in sermon preparation, you must have more ideas and suggestions stored away than you are ever likely to use. All this presupposes much reading and study. You must be full yourselves before you can share with others. You cannot get water from an empty well.

So what do you study? The Bible of course; theology; science; psychology; biography; great novels; poems and plays … all these will help to fill your minds and notebooks with the material from which your sermons will be made. And not only books, but people. If your sermons are to be alive, human, full of interest, you must study people, for human nature is the material with which you deal. Know it through and through. People's likes and dislikes, their successes and failures, their loves and hates, their joys and sorrows.

Read the parables of Jesus and see how many of them came from His knowledge of people. The hasty scrambling for the chief seats; the searching for the lost coin; the shepherd seeking his lost sheep; the farmer sowing seeds; the merchant and his pearls …. Read and study and keep the storehouse full.

New preachers may find it easy to prepare their first sermon. Excited and ardent, they find thoughts springing spontaneously to their minds. With this experience they imagine it will be continually easy to prepare sermons. They do not always realise that in this first sermon they are drawing on all they have thought, read, seen, heard and experienced since childhood. They are like a man who has inherited a fortune and spends it recklessly. The store is gradually diminished, depleted, and they wonder why the preparation of further sermons is so difficult.

The homiletic mind

It is not only *what* you read either in books or human nature, but *how* you read that counts. Again, look at Jesus' teaching. How many people had seen a farmer sowing seeds; or a shepherd seeking a lost sheep; or children playing in the street? To them these were just ordinary experiences of life. But to Jesus they were something more. These were experiences that could be used to illustrate some great truths about God.

So, as you read, see, and hear, extract the significance of things. Ideas, suggestions, illustrations, themes. All lie to hand for the taking if you have eyes to see and ears to hear. These are the seed thoughts from which future sermons will grow. Capture them before they are lost.

When reading a book or a newspaper, listening to the radio or watching television and something strikes you - an idea, a topic, or an illustration - make a note of it. Keep these seed thoughts safe and they will grow.

How to plant

A useful method of filing material for future use is to use several different envelopes. It is quick, easy and cheap. The envelope should be fairly large. Tearing off the flaps, and slitting down the right-hand sides, makes an easy way of depositing and withdrawing notes. The principle is one subject, one envelope. Keep all your cuttings; notes; book references; everything that has a bearing on the subject. For example: Providence; Sacrifice; Evangelism etc. are placed in the respective envelope. The envelopes can be placed upright between bookends and take up very little room. If alphabetical guides are used, any subject can be found at a glance.

Having deposited the first few seedlings let them grow. Day by day, as you find seed thoughts applicable to a subject, plant them in the envelope concerned. Let them stay there for days, weeks, even months. Then one day, when you want to speak on a certain subject, you pull out your envelope and you will be surprised to find out how much material you have accumulated. If, in browsing over the contents of your envelope you come across any cuttings that have become out-of-date, you can discard them without affecting the rest of the material.

Plagiarism

You have to be careful how you use other people's thoughts, for it might easily lead to plagiarism, which is literary theft. If you use quotations verbatim, you must acknowledge the source from which they come. You cannot take other people's work and pass it off as your own. However, no-one can be completely original in thought. Everyone feeds on other people's concepts. Ideas are universal. Originality lies not in the ideas themselves, but in the selection and arrangement of ideas and facts. You gather the facts, illustrations, concepts, ideas, and from this mixture strive to bring some kind of unity. Ideas are collected from all kinds of different sources, but they must be shaped by your own thinking and tested by your own experience. As Spurgeon put it: "I cannot wear another man's coat; it would not fit me. But this is what I do. I tear it to pieces and make a waistcoat of it."

This, then, is the truth of the matter. You must borrow ideas, facts, thoughts, concepts, if your own thinking is to be stimulated. But acknowledge what you borrow, and having passed it through the crucible of your own mind, make your own waistcoat.

Let it simmer

You have plenty of material stored away in your envelope. This is the material from which you will make your sermon. But it is a jumble, all higgledy-piggledy. A strange conglomeration of texts, bits of verse, quotations, illustrations, newspaper cuttings, book references, and the fruit of your own thinking. Now is the time to take things quietly. You must meditate and brood. Do not be in too great a rush to begin your sermon. Let your mind be in a receptive condition as you ponder over the mass of material. Before you write a word of the sermon let the material speak to you. Let it 'stew' in your mind. Mull it over. Let it simmer. It is amazing what new ideas this simmering will bring to the top.

This is the period of incubation. It is during this period that the subconscious mind takes over and helps in the work of creative thinking. There is a kind of unconscious concentration which seizes upon the ideas, and rejects, selects, arranges, unifies, until at length all that is left to do is the actual work of writing. Also during this period, in which the main theme of the sermon 'gels', you come to the rest of your preparation being able to say, "This is what I am going to preach about."

Association of ideas

In your period of simmering, ideas subconsciously associate with one another, so that at the end of your brooding, you have far more ideas than you had when you started. Let me, with diffidence, offer a couple of examples from my own efforts.

(1) Saved by the Bible

I once read a newspaper report of an American airman who was on a raid over Germany during the war. A fragment of flak tore through his leather jacket and lodged in a steel covered Bible he wore in his breast pocket. This undoubtedly saved his life. In the report a suggestion was made that such a Bible should be supplied to every service man to give protection in battle.

The association was easy here. Saved by the Bible. Salvation through the Word of God. But what about the suggestion? Did it not savour of credulity or superstition? It could lead to the unreasonable belief that if you carry a Bible in your pocket, you are safe.

You know better than that. It is in your heart, not just in your pocket, that you want your Bible. This gave me my text. "I have hidden your word in my heart." (Psalm 119 v.11).

Who gave him the Bible? Was it his parents, his Sunday School teacher? His youth group leader? And why was it given? Not just to wear but to use. He would need this Bible to nourish his faith in the strange experiences he would face. Away from all the good influences of his church, family and friends, he would need the Bible to give him guidance. He would need happiness. Much of what he would find would be shallow, trivial, tawdry; pleasures snatched at between periods of stress and strain. All he needed in the way of nourishment, guidance and strength he would find in the Bible.

I let the ideas simmer and then, taking the text mentioned, preached the sermon "Saved by the Bible." *[In due course this illustration was reused for one of the Radio 4 meditations "Breakfast for the Mind", see Part 3, p.124 - Ed.]*

(2) Handicapped heroes

I had been reading tributes to President Roosevelt. His leadership, his courage, his championship of the poor, his love of freedom, his work as a great leader in the time of war. It was pointed out, however, that his true greatness was shown not merely in these things; but that he was this kind of man and rendered this kind of service in spite of a severe handicap.

Endowed with a famous name, already having held high office, he was recognised as one of the leaders of his party and nation. Then, with swift suddenness, at the age of thirty-nine, when all the signs were set fair for a brilliant career, he was stricken with infantile paralysis which left his body palsied from the hips down.

Confined to a wheelchair, one would not have been surprised if he had given up all hope of public service and taken life easily. He had adequate financial resources. But he would not give up. In the curative waters of Warm Springs he partly conquered his malady by swimming (at first with his arms only), until his legs, aided by crutches, became strong enough to bear his weight. Thus handicapped, he plunged once more into the service of his fellows with zeal and self dedication.

Reading these tributes was enough to bring back to my mind other heroes who, in spite of disability, endured to the end. Roosevelt amongst the statesmen; blind Milton and consumptive Stevenson among the poets and writers; Beethoven with his deafness among the musicians; Ignatius Loyola, crippled, founder of "The Society of Jesus" among the missionary pioneers; Helen Keller, blind, deaf, and dumb, among those who worked for the relief of the suffering. *[This was used in another Radio 4 meditation, p.116 - Ed.]*

Another hero with a disability was the apostle Paul. That bold, adventurous, fearless man, spending his life in the service of his fellows and his God. He, too, had a handicap. No-one knows exactly what he meant by the words he used to describe it - "a thorn in the flesh". There are those who suggest it was a moral and spiritual trouble from which he suffered - some agonising conflict with conscience. Most authorities, however, are of the opinion that the words meant some physical form of suffering - some infirmity of the body.

One suggestion is that he was subject to epileptic fits; another, that he had serious trouble with his eyes following the blindness that came upon him on the Damascus road. Whatever it was, the word picture describing his suffering shows that it was excruciatingly painful.

This health-shattered apostle, doing his work for Christ, adding to his suffering by shipwrecks, stripes and imprisonment, presents a picture of greatness.

As we reflect upon the characters of such people, refusing to let the hardships of life get them down, facing life bravely; moulding their lives rather than being moulded by circumstances; not merely enduring, but conquering; we ourselves are shamed, challenged and encouraged.

Such a sermon was worth preaching, and I called it *"Handicapped Heroes"*, taking for my text "I was given a thorn in my flesh." (2 Corinthians 12 v.7).

I mention these two examples, not because I believe them to be outstanding in any way, but to show how, through association of ideas, a preacher may be able to light their own fire from the fires of others.

Chapter 2 : Topics, Themes, Texts & Titles

There is a difference between these terms. The *topic* is the particular phrase or aspect of the general subject with which you are to deal in the sermon.

The *theme* is the gist of the sermon - what the sermon is about.

The *text* is the verse or passage of scripture which relates to the particular aspect of the subject you are dealing with in your sermon.

The *title* is the label you give to the completed sermon. This describes the sermon, and helps to attract attention and to create interest.

A few examples may help to make these distinctions clear.

Example one

SUBJECT: (broad general field) Prayer.

TOPIC: (special aspect) The problem of prayer.

THEME: (what the sermon is about) This sermon deals with some of the difficulties of prayer, and how they may be overcome.

TEXT: "Pray continually" (1 Thessalonians 5 v.17).

TITLE: (description) If through regular prayer you overcome your difficulties, then the title can be "Kneel to Conquer".

Example two

SUBJECT: Evangelism

TOPIC: A special mission, either forthcoming or just over.

THEME: The sermon deals with the excitement and joy to be found in the work of evangelism.

TEXT: "The seventy-two returned with joy" (Luke 10 v.17)

TITLE: "The Exhilaration of Evangelism".

At the beginning of every sermon ask yourself four questions.

1) What am I going to preach about? (Topic) Example: "The importance of the Spiritual".

2) What am I going to say about it? (Theme) Example: I am going to point out that we are spoiling our lives and losing our moral and spiritual freedom because we neglect the spiritual, and put our trust in material things.

3) What passage of Scripture am I going to use? (Text) Example: "Is not life more than food?" (Matthew 6 v.25).

4) How am I going to describe it? (Title) Example: "Life and Livelihood".

Should you use texts?

From the point of view of preaching, the word 'text' has come to stand for the verse or passage of Scripture which is used as the theme of the discourse. The word derives from the Latin 'texere', 'to weave'. Texts contain strands of truth which are taken from the Scriptures and woven into the sermon.

Yet, it isn't always easy to find an appropriate text for your sermon. Spurgeon, for example, confessed that finding a text had frequently been a burden to him. He asked his grandfather, who had been in the ministry for over fifty years, whether he was ever perplexed in this way. The old man confessed that sometimes he was. "The difficulty," he said, "was not that there are not enough texts, but that there are so many."

Spurgeon states that he could spend more time praying and waiting for the right text than preparing his sermon. He would continue to make outlines on this text and the other until at last one gripped him. Then he knew that this was his text. He tells how, when living in Cambridge, he had to preach in a neighbouring village one evening. He had spent most of the day turning from one verse to another, but "his mind would not take hold". He happened to look out of the window. On the other side of the street he saw a poor, solitary canary upon the tiles, surrounded by a crowd of sparrows who were pecking at it as though they would tear it to pieces. At once a verse came to his mind. "Has not my inheritance become to me like a speckled bird of prey that other birds of prey surround and attack?" (Jeremiah 12 v.9). He walked to the village chapel, meditating upon the text, and preached "with freedom and ease to myself, and, I believe, with comfort to my rustic audience upon the peculiar people and their persecution by their enemies." But Spurgeon had to know his Bible to think of a text like that!!

Prodding and probing

Before making any use of a text you must be sure you know what it really means. You must probe and prod until you have discovered the exact truth the text contains. This is where you must consult various versions and commentaries. Such consultations will reveal to you the finer shades of meaning the texts contain.

Take an example: in the Authorised version, 2 Corinthians 3 v.18 reads "But we all, with open face, beholding as in a glass the glory of the Lord, are changed into the same image from glory to glory even as by the Spirit of the Lord."

The translators used the words "beholding as in a glass" because they thought that Paul meant that the face of Jesus Christ is like a mirror in which we can see God. This, of course is true. We do know what God is like by looking at Jesus. He is a mirror reflecting God to us. "Philip said, 'Lord, show us the Father.' Jesus answered: 'Anyone who has seen me has seen the Father.'" (John 14 vv.8-9). But although this is true, this is not what Paul was talking about. Moffat translates the words: "But we all mirror the glory." The New English Bible uses, "We all reflect as in a mirror." The Living Bible translates: "We can be mirrors that brightly reflect." The Good News Bible states: "All of us, then, reflect the glory of the Lord."

There is a difference here that is vital. One idea is that people look to Jesus to see a reflection of God; the other idea is that they themselves are mirrors reflecting the glory of God. Both conceptions are true. It is the second one, however, that concerned Paul in his letter. Without checking the other translations you would miss Paul's real thought.

Next, you need to study the context. A study of the background helps us to discover the truth enshrined in the text. In addition, you must draw out of the text the meaning that is actually there, not what you think is there. Ask questions:- How? Why? What? Where? Who? Who said the words? Why were they said? When were they said? Were they true then? Are they appropriate today? Do the words contain some fundamental principle that will always be relevant?

Asking questions of the text, comparing the various versions, studying the context - in all these ways you dig down until you discover the truth.

How to use texts

There are many ways of dealing with a single text. Having probed, prodded, asked questions, taken due note of the context, and being persuaded you have come as near as you can to the pith of the text, simply expound this truth, explain it, and present the implications for your hearers.

Alternatively, having grasped the essential truth, having discovered the philosophical principle of which the text is an expression, use that as the theme of the sermon. Then preach upon that theme. For example: in the story of the threatened destruction of Sodom, we find Abraham questioning God: "Will you sweep away the righteous with the wicked? ... Far be it from you! Will not the Judge of all the earth do right?" (Genesis 18 vv.23-25). Here the theme arises naturally from the text - "That our moral sense depends upon our innate conviction of the righteousness of God's rule." Having used the text to introduce the theme, it is now perfectly legitimate to make the theme the main thing.

Another way is to hold up the text as a jewel. Turn it round and round so that the light plays first on this facet, then on that. Each facet will catch and reflect the light.

It is occasionally of value to use more than one text, sometimes complementary, sometimes contrasting.

Example 1:

1) "Where is the lamb for the burnt offering?" (Genesis 22 v.7).

2) "Look, the Lamb of God" (John 1 v.29).

3) "Worthy is the Lamb, who was slain ..." (Revelation 5 v.12).

Example 2:

1) "Forget the former things; do not dwell on the past."
(Isaiah 43 v.18).

2) "Remember the former things, those of long ago."
(Isaiah 46 v.9).

Example 3:

1) "For each one should carry their own load." (Galatians 6 v.5).

2) "Carry each other's burdens" (Galatians 6 v.2).

3) "Cast your cares on the Lord." (Psalm 55 v.22).

In the third example, the first text speaks of our own need of courage in facing life; the second reminds us of the duty and privilege of sympathy and service; the third, our dependence upon God for strength to bear our own burdens and to help our fellows.

For a sermon on *"Progress in Discipleship"*, I once used:

1) "Come to me ..." (Matthew 11 v.28).

2) "Learn from me ..." (Matthew 11 v.29).

3) "Come, follow me ..." (Matthew 4 v.19).

One sermon I enjoyed preparing and preaching was called *"The Three Gardens"*.

1) "Now the Lord God had planted a garden in the east, in Eden." (Genesis 2 v.8).

2) "Jesus … crossed the Kidron Valley. On the other side there was a garden" (John 18 v.1).

3) "At the place where Jesus was crucified, there was a garden." (John 19 v.41).

I once used five texts for a sermon. Entitled *"This One Thing"*, the texts I used were:

1) "One thing I ask from the Lord." (Psalm 27 v.4).

2) "One thing you lack." (Mark 10 v.21).

3) "You are worried and upset about many things, but few things are needed - or indeed only one." (Luke 10 vv.41,42).

4) "One thing I do know." (John 9 v.25).

5) "But one thing I do:" (Philippians 3 v.13).

Another time when I used five texts was for a sermon during a Parliamentary election. Entitled *"The Church's Manifesto"*, I took up the points dealt with by the candidates:

1) PEACE: "Peace I leave with you." (John 14 v.27).

2) HOUSING: "My Father's house has many rooms." (John 14 v.2).

3) SECURITY: "The eternal God is your refuge, and underneath are the everlasting arms." (Deuteronomy 33 v.27).

4) EDUCATION: "Learn from me." (Matthew 11 v.29).

5) FOREIGN POLICY: "Therefore go and make disciples of all nations …" (Matthew 28 v.19).

Other examples could be given with multiple texts, (contrasting, complementary, developing) but sufficient have been given to show the advantage of using more than one text for a sermon. One need not use this idea too often, but to attempt it occasionally is exciting both for preacher and congregation.

Necessity of topics, themes and titles

A sermon may not have a text, but it must have a topic, a theme and a title. The topic is what you are going to speak about; the theme is what you are going to say about it; and the title is the name of the finished product. The purpose of all three is to give point and direction to the sermon; to keep the sermon on the main track.

I once preached in a church where the first thing I saw when I entered the pulpit was a card on the book-rest which read, "Sir, we would see Jesus." That card was a reminder to any preacher as to what his aim ought to be in preaching.

Which should come first - text, topic or theme? Sometimes the one, sometimes the other. It does not really matter. Whichever you start from you really do the same thing. If you come across a text that grips you, find the purpose of the text, the truth it enshrines, then write down that truth in a brief sentence or paragraph. On the other hand, if you light upon a topic or theme first, find a text which contains the truth which these declare.

For example, taking the text first, suppose you wished to preach upon the parable of the Prodigal Son. Here there are so many truths that, unless you select one aspect of the parable and preach on that, your sermon is apt to be too general and vague.

Suppose you took the part where the Prodigal "Came to his senses" and realised his wretched position (Luke 15 v.17). What are you going to say about it? You say what the Prodigal realised - that his lifestyle was too expensive. He could not afford to live like that. It was spoiling his life. So, in a sentence here is the theme: "The High Cost of Low Living is too Expensive."

Repeating this theme at intervals during the delivery would surely make it memorable to the congregation.

Sometimes you find the theme first. I remember reading an article in a magazine on the value of man from the point of view of an analytical chemist. The article revealed that a man's body contained enough fat to make a few bars of soap; enough iron to make a nail; enough sugar to fill one saucer; enough lime to wash a hen-coop; enough phosphorous to point a few dozen matches; enough magnesium to supply one dose of medicine. This gave me my topic. How much is a man really worth?

It struck me that there were differing standards of judgement. Besides that of the analytical chemist, who made a physical judgement, there was the estimate of the man's employer who based his judgement on the amount of time and labour expended in his service. There is the estimate of the general public whose basis of judgement is possessions. "How much was he worth?" they ask when a man dies and his will is published.

But there is also the standpoint of religion, which takes into account a man's soul, which other estimates neglect. Here, then, is the theme. An attempt to answer the question from varying standards of judgement, leading to the answer given by religion.

What about the text? I found it in Romans: "But God demonstrates his own love for us in this: While we were still sinners, Christ died for us." (Romans 5 v.8). That is the worth of man. He is worth dying for. I preached that sermon at a Good Friday service.

Little has been said so far about titles. The function of a title is to give a name to the sermon. It also shares with topic and theme the purpose of clarifying the mind of the preacher and making doubly sure that the sermon has a definite aim. Titles should be clear, accurate, comprehensive, interesting, and attractive. For example, one of my sermons referred to earlier:

Title: *"The Exhilaration of Evangelism"*

Text: "The seventy-two returned with joy." (Luke 10 v.17).

A further fruitful source of titles, topics or themes is the hymn book. For example, John Ernest Bode's hymn:

> *O Jesus I have promised*
> *To serve thee to the end ...*

The text is the hymn itself; the title a line from the hymn, "I have promised". The theme, also unmistakably and clearly expressed in the hymn: "The central act of religion is the act of commitment."

Or Robert Grant's hymn:

> *O worship the King,*
> *All glorious above;*
> *O gratefully sing*
> *His power and His love.*

I have used this hymn as follows: the fourth line of the first verse gave the title *"His power and His Love."* The topic was "The Contrasting and Complementary Attributes of God." For the text I went to the Psalms: "He heals the brokenhearted and binds up their wounds. He determines the number of the stars and calls them each by name." (Psalm 147 vv.3&4). The theme: We cannot separate the attributes of God. However contradictory they may seem, they are not mutually exclusive. Both conceptions, transcendence and immanence, must be held together. Power and love, might and mercy, stars and sympathy, belong together. "Lord, if you are willing, you can make me clean." said the leper (Matthew 8 v.2), acknowledging the power but doubting the love. "But if you can do anything, take pity on us and help us." (Mark 9 v.22), cried the desperate father, acknowledging the love, but doubting the power. God is both able and willing. That was the theme.

Topics, themes, texts and titles. Sometimes they come in a flash. Sometimes as the result of hard thinking. But these must be settled before you begin to give the sermon outline or form. It is the discovery of these that gives sermon-making its thrill and excitement.

Chapter 3 : The Sermon Structure

Topic, theme, text and title having been settled, the time has now come to give some thought to the shape of the sermon. Having decided *what* you are going to speak about, and what you are going to say about it, you must now decide *how* you are going to say it. In other words, you need to prepare a plan, a scheme, an outline, of the sermon.

Listening to the sermons of some lay preachers it is obvious that this is the part of the preparation they have scrimped. They have excellent material, but very little order, shape or balance. It is not only what you say, but also how you say it, which makes an effective sermon. An outline aids you in the development of your thought. It keeps you on the right track. It ensures that each part of your sermon is in the right proportion. Moreover, a well thought out plan makes the sermon easier for the congregation to listen to, easier to understand, and easier to remember.

The aim determines the outline

The outline must be determined by the type of sermon you have in mind. A builder's plan will depend upon whether the building is to be a castle or a cottage. The same materials will be used but different plans are required. So too in sermon preparation. The plan will depend on the purpose and aim of the sermon. Use the type of structure most suited to your theme, whether it be the interpretation of a text, the treatment of a social problem, the presentation of a particular doctrine, or a sermon on the development of the spiritual life.

The three column method

One method I used a great deal in my earlier ministry was what I may describe as "The Three Column Method." In this method you take a large sheet of paper and mark out three columns. Now you get your envelope with 20, 30, 40, suggestions, ideas, illustrations, quotations etc. Number them, just as they come to hand and put the numbers down in the first column, higgledy-piggledy, without any form or order.

Each number represents a brick for the building of your sermon. There will be too many for one sermon, some of them the wrong shape and size. But better to have too many than too few. The bricks you discard can be used for the building of another sermon.

Now concentrate on the first column. You will find that some of the numbers represent ideas and thoughts that obviously belong together. So you will take from the first column those ideas which are obviously related and put them in groups in column two.

Now you have three, four, or five groups in the second column, with three, four, or five items in each group. Next give suitable headings to each group, and you are getting on well with you structure.

Concentrate now on column two. Decide in what order these groups must be used. One must obviously be used as a starting point. Put this at the top of column three. Then let the other groups follow naturally and logically. This will take time and concentration, but you will find it well worth while. Having sorted out the groups in order in this way, you will now have your outline before you. You can stop here if you wish, and use the outline as the sermon, or you can use it as the basis and write out the sermon in full.

Discovering a unifying thought in a text

You can base an outline on the flow, the movement, the development of a text. For example, in Peter's sermon at Pentecost (Acts 2 vv.14-31) the movement is from the past to the present, from prophecy to fulfilment.

Sometimes the movement is from theory to practice. Paul's letter to the Romans develops in this way. The theory, the doctrine, coming in the first eleven chapters, and the flow from theology to practice coming in the first verse of chapter 12: "Therefore, I urge you, brothers and sisters ..." (Romans 12 v.1).

Sometimes the movement is from the divine to the human; the human to the divine; the particular to the general; the general to the particular. According to the movement of the text, so the plan is prepared.

Variety

It is important to try to obtain variety in the structure of your sermons. Here are examples of five possible classifications.

(a) Exposition

Here you set out to explain a passage of Scripture. It can take the form of a single text, a chapter, or a book. True expository preaching is not merely verse by verse commentary. If you are going to show the congregation what a passage of Scripture really means, then some sort of structure or plan is bound to be helpful. For example, the Lord's Prayer can be outlined as:

1) An Address to God;

2) A Petition for God's Reign Over All;

3) A Prayer for Ourselves;

4) Ascription of Praise.

What has been called "Paul's Hymn To Love" can be treated similarly (1Corinthians 13).

1) The Importance of Love (vv.1-3).

2) The Characteristics of Love (vv.4-7).

3) The Permanence of Love (vv.8-13).

(b) Argument

Here a thesis, a principle of truth is expounded, and the sermon sets out to establish these statements by logical argument. There are two methods which can be used under this heading: *deductive* and *inductive*. Deduction means applying a general principle to individual instances. For example, a preacher, conducting a mission service, may take for a text the general statement, "All have sinned and fall short of the glory of God," (Romans 3 v.23).

Proceeding from this general truth it could be applied to individual instances, showing how even the best of men, including examples from the Bible and history, would come under this condemnation. Next the truth could be applied to the congregation, and an appeal made to trust in a Saviour for salvation.

Induction means working from individual instances and discovering some general and universal principle. As an example the preacher could take as a theme something like, "Would it be good if all prayers were answered? Would the answer always be welcome?"

Isaiah, Augustine, St. Francis, David Livingstone, John Wesley and others have all left it on record that they have been troubled when God answered their prayers. It is all very well to pray for light and guidance, but suppose the answer is disturbing? Suppose the guidance leads to the path of danger? This is sometimes - often - true. Is it good to have our prayers answered? What about the disturbance, the pain, the danger, the answer may bring? The more you delve into individual instances, the more you find a common testimony. It is worthwhile enduring the pain to get the answer.

(c) Faceting and categorising

In *faceting* you hold up the text as though it were a gem, and let the light shine upon each facet. For example, take Thomas' absence from the Upper Room when Jesus appeared. (John 20 vv.19-24). Hold that up. Let the light shine upon it. Twist the jewel around, this way and that.

What did Thomas lose by being absent?

He missed the PRESENCE. "Jesus came and stood among them."

He missed the PEACE. "Peace be with you."

He missed the PROJECT. "I am sending you."

He missed the POWER. "Receive the Holy Spirit."

He missed the PLEASURE - although 'pleasure' is too weak a word for the happiness and rapture which filled their hearts: "The disciples were overjoyed when they saw the Lord."

Categorising is applying the text to various categories, sections or classes. I once preached a sermon on the topic "Are the teachings of Jesus out-of-date?" In endeavouring to answer this question I discussed what Jesus taught about:

1) The Religious Life.   2) The Social Life.

3) The Individual Life.

I then compared the teaching of Jesus in these various categories with that of modern teachers, showing that far from Jesus being out-of-date, modern educators have not yet caught up with His teaching.

(d) Analogy

In this method of planning you use an illustration and carry out that illustration as the structure of the sermon. Paul does this when he uses the running of a race to describe the living of the Christian life. He takes his illustration from the Greek Games and explores the comparison and similarities as he urges those to whom he is writing to learn a lesson from the contestants (1 Corinthians 9 vv.24-27).

(1) Contest

The race is a Contest. The Christian Life is a Contest.

(2) Conditions

(a) Moral Test. In the Games no cheating is allowed. Compare this with the Oath taken at the modern Olympic Games. The moral test is for the contestants, not the spectators. There is a moral test in the Christian Life. This is applied to disciples, not unbelievers.

(b) Physical Test. Striving, agonising. Training could not be broken. Body under subjection. So in the Christian life for the disciples, hungering and thirsting after righteousness.

(3) Crown

For the contestants a corruptible crown. For the Christian, an incorruptible crown.

(e) Another example

There is a method deriving from the Hegelian philosophy which revolves around three ideas: thesis; antithesis, and synthesis.

First, you state a fact or a truth (thesis); then you state the opposite (anti-thesis); then you conclude with the truth emerging from the combination of these contradictory statements.

A story of a Welsh minister illustrates this method. One or two of his Welsh members had married English wives. He preached in Welsh, but for the sake of the wives gave the outline of his sermon in English so that they would know what he was talking about. Sometimes he found this a little difficult. He thought in Welsh, but had to translate into English.

In preaching one sermon his first point was the condition of the world as it actually was (thesis). His second point was the condition of an ideal world, the world as it ought to be (anti-thesis). His third point was that the first picture could be turned into the second picture (the actual into the ideal) through the instrumentality of the Church (synthesis).

He could say this in Welsh, but found it more difficult in English. This is how he managed it:-

1) The world upside down.   2) The world downside up.

3) And we're the boys to do it!

A method attributed to many famous names is the following:- "First, I tell them what I'm going to tell them; then I tell them; then I tell them what I've told them."

Essentials of a plan

Whatever your method of planning a sermon - and there must be variety - there are basic essentials which are common to all.

(1) The plan must have unity. To achieve unity, each point must be subordinate to the main theme. Three detached sermonettes do not make one sermon. Neither do a handful of observations tied together by a text make an organic whole. There must be unity. One theme, one thing you want to say, one truth you want to declare, however many arguments or illustrations you use.

(2) There must also be proportion. This does not mean that each sub-heading is necessarily of the same length, but that each is proportionately related to the main theme and to each other.

(3) With unity and proportion, there must be progression. There must be a sense of advancement, movement, logical progress. The points must develop from one another, progressing till the sermon is finished and you have reached the climax.

Chapter 4 : Introductions and Conclusions

Why an introduction?

First of all because of one of the oldest rules in preaching: "Begin well and end well". But how are you to begin well? Remember, this is the first part of the sermon the congregation hears. It will often depend upon the introduction whether or not they will listen to any other part of the discourse. The purpose of the introduction is to gain the goodwill of the listener and to arouse interest in the theme. It is to let the congregation know what the sermon is about, and to prepare them to understand it.

When preparing an introduction the preacher must remember two things:

(1) They must *really* introduce. Both theme and audience must be brought together. This is the journey they will take together. This is how they will travel.

(2) They must *only* introduce. Their purpose is to create interest, not to satiate.

When is the best time to prepare the introductions? Some say that, although being the first to be spoken, it must be the last to be written. You must know a person before you can introduce him to someone else. A preacher must know the sermon before being able to introduce it to the congregation.

Biblical examples

You may not be able to start exactly like the great figures of the Bible, but take notice how they demanded attention in their introductions. There was a sense of urgency, of consequence, of importance, in their opening words.

Listen to Isaiah: "Therefore hear the word of the Lord, you scoffers who rule this people in Jerusalem." (Isaiah 28 v.14). Or listen to Stephen: "Brothers and fathers, listen to me!" (Acts 7 v.2). Again, listen to Jesus: "Jesus called the crowd to him and said, 'Listen and understand.'" (Matthew 15 v.10).

So they compelled attention. You may not be able to use the same words, but something of the concern, importance and significance of your message must characterise your introductions. Whatever words you use, you must give the impression of saying "I have something to say to you ... Listen!"

You must use your introduction to present the problem, setting, character of your theme swiftly. Whatever style of introduction you use, the audience must know what you are going to talk about in the first few sentences.

This was how Jesus worked. Take the parable of the Prodigal Son. Here is the opening: "There was a man who had two sons. The younger one said to his father, 'Father, give me my share of the estate.'" (Luke 15 vv.11-12).

Or this: "Two men went up to the temple to pray, one a Pharisee and the other a tax collector." (Luke 18 v.10).

Study these two examples. It is all there. Central characters, number of characters, problem, atmosphere, suspense - all in a sentence or two.

That is what you must aim at in your introductions. You must set out the essence of what you want to say. Invite and compel the interest and attention of your hearers. There are sluggish minds that need to be brought into alertness, and wandering thoughts that must be brought into focus.

Start with a bang!

Begin with a brief, terse sentence or two that pulls the congregation up with a start. I once began a sermon by saying, "I have preached in churches and mission halls; in a busy street; on a quiet country green; and on the sea shore. I have preached in innumerable places, but I have never had to begin by saying, 'I'm not drunk!'" Peter did! (Acts 2 v.15).

But there is a danger that startling openings, unexpected statements, starting with a bang, raises the expectation of the congregation to such an extent that the rest of the sermon will fall seriously below such a level.

Texts and contexts

Perhaps the most common method of introducing a sermon is to deal with the text itself. To set it forth in historical background; to show it clearly in its context; to show its relationship with topic and title; and to show the new light that is thrown upon the truth by a comparison of various versions. Some might ask what has such historical background got to do with the man in the pew? It is not what happened in Biblical times but what is happening in present day life that needs to be dealt with. But there are times when understanding the historical setting, relating the text to the context, comparing the various versions, will make the relevance of the text stand out with sharpness and vividness, and make the relevance of the text doubly clear.

Once I wanted to preach a sermon dealing with the narrowness and prejudice shown by people in matters of race relationships, and the narrow intolerance shown in matters of denominationalism. I chose the text, "You are well aware that it is against our law for a Jew to associate with or visit a Gentile. But God has shown me that I should not call anyone impure or unclean." (Acts 10 v.28). I began with the text and the context.

Two men had visions. The one, a Gentile, Cornelius, the Roman centurion; the other, a Jew, Peter the apostle. The result of these visions was that barriers were broken down, tradition was discovered to be false, truth was born in the soul, the Gospel was set free from limitations, and a step forward was taken towards the true brotherhood of man.

The account of these visions and their result is dealt with at great length in this chapter. This is not surprising as the incidents recorded were of the utmost importance in the growth of the early church. They represented a new departure, the overcoming of narrow-mindedness and prejudice of the Jewish-Christian thought.

The crux of the chapter lies in the verse which forms our text. Here Peter makes a two-fold declaration. "You are well aware that it is against our law for a Jew to associate with or visit a Gentile." This is the first part, describing an old tradition. "But God has shown me that I should not call anyone impure or unclean." (Acts 10 v.28) This is the second part, describing new truth. The bridge that spanned the gulf between the old and the new, between tradition and truth, was the vision Peter received at Joppa. "God has shown me …"

Today's news is full of racial hatred and wars between nations. No-one could say that such a text, and its context, is irrelevant.

Quotations

Here a preacher quotes a statement of truth, or some striking sentence which illustrates his title or contains the truth of the sermon's theme.

"Does God Care?" Is that the theme? What about Thomas Hardy's ending of his book *'Tess of the Durbervilles'* - "The President of the Immortals had ended his sport with Tess."? A magnificent sentence to end a book. A splendid quotation to begin a sermon on this topic. What a picture of God. God playing with the lives of men as a chessman plays with his pieces, and tiring of the game, shuts the board and sends all the pieces flying. Is God like that?

In your general reading some striking sentence will suddenly shine out as though it were illuminated. Having seized upon your mind, there is every chance that it will have an equal effect upon others when used as an introduction.

Statement of purpose

Occasionally, the main outline of the sermon can be given as the introduction. After announcing the text, the preacher says, "I desire in this sermon to establish the following points: (1) So-and-so; (2) So-and-so; (3) So-and-so.

Following this type of introduction, here is one I gave in a sermon to Sunday School Teachers. *[See Part 3, p.137, "Teach Your Children" - Ed.]* The text was: "Only be careful, and watch yourselves closely so that you do not forget the things your eyes have seen or let them fade from your heart as long as you live. Teach them to your children and to their children after them." (Deuteronomy 4 v.9).

This text has something to say about the teaching of children. This is our task. There are three profound questions asked and answered by the text:

(1) Who are we to teach? "Your children and grandchildren.

(2) What are we to teach? This is contained in the chapter - laws; commandments; the story of deliverance; but especially "Remember the day you stood before the Lord your God at Horeb." (Deuteronomy 4 v.9). Your own personal experience of God.

(3) Why are we to teach? "So that they will learn to obey me as long as they live, and so that they will teach their children to do the same."

Illustrations

Illustrative material, especially news items, can be used for interesting and captivating introductions to sermons, especially for topical sermons.

I have already referred to a newspaper report of an American airman whose life was saved by a steel-covered Bible which he wore in his breast pocket. This item, used as an introduction, gave the topic of the sermon: "Saved by the Bible."

Another example: I came across an old story about two Scots, Angus and Donald. They had known each other all their lives, but many years ago, when they were young men, some stupid quarrel had ruptured their friendship. Although living in the same village, ever since that day, they had had no dealings with one another. When both were old men, Angus became seriously ill and likely to die. He felt he could not die without being reconciled to his one-time friend. Donald was sent for and he came to the bedside of the sick man. Angus told of his desire. There was a moment's pause, then Donald said, "Give us your hand."

Solemnly the two stubborn men shook hands, After a moment Angus asked, "It's all right now, Donald?" "Aye", replied Donald. "It's all right now. But mind ye, if you're no dead by the morning, it's no all right yet!"

I used this story as an introduction to the question, "Lord, how many times shall I forgive my brother or sister who sins against me? Up to seven times?" (Matthew 18 v.21). My title was "The Spirit of Forgiveness." Can that spirit be one of cold calculation? Is it forgiveness when it is carefully measured out - so much and no more?

Conclusions

Equally important as Introductions are Conclusions. Some preachers make the conclusion the first item of their preparation. A sermon is like a journey. You want to arrive somewhere. You have a destination. Make sure you know where you want to go. The concluding words of a sermon must leave the congregation with a clear and memorable impression.

Here are five methods of concluding a sermon.

(a) Recapitulation

You give a brief summary of what has been said, finishing with a final sentence which lodges the whole truth of the sermon in the mind of the congregation.

Here is a conclusion I used in preaching a sermon on Peter's suggestion on the Mount of Transfiguration: "Lord, it is good for us to be here. If you wish, I will put up three shelters - one for you, one for Moses and one for Elijah."
(Matthew 17 v.4).

"We cannot linger too long in the sanctuary, for outside is the world and its need. Worship and work go hand in hand. It is not sufficient to be on the mountain top, however satisfying, unless we are willing to descend to the valley. Equally, we shall be of little use in the valley, unless we have shared the experience of the mountain top. The vision of the mountain must be taken to the valley; the spirit of the sanctuary must be taken into our daily lives."

There is much to be said for a simple recapitulation to conclude the sermon.

(b) Personal appeal

All great preachers whose words have really affected hearts and lives have used the direct personal appeal.

How could anyone have answered other than the Israelites did when Joshua made his appeal at the assembly at Shechem? "Now fear the Lord and serve him with all faithfulness ... choose for yourselves this day whom you will serve .... The people then said to Joshua 'We will serve the Lord our God and obey him.'" (Joshua 24 vv.14,15,24).

Is there anything more haunting than the appeal of Jesus, "Come to me, all you who are weary and burdened, and I will give you rest." (Matthew 11 v.28) ?

It was by way of personal appeal that preachers like Spurgeon concluded their sermons. Preaching on the children of Ephraim turning back in the day of battle (Psalm 78 v.9), Spurgeon concluded, "May God's eternal mercy seek and save you, and if it be His will, may He find you, and lead you to put your trust in Jesus Christ, and resting on Him, and looking to His cross, you shall not, as the children of Ephraim did, 'turn back in the day of battle.'"

Spurgeon again: a sermon on the text, "The Spirit and the bride say, 'Come!' And let the one who hears say, 'Come!' Let the one who is thirsty come; and let the one who wishes take the free gift of the water of life." (Revelation 22 v.17).

"Shall I preach in vain? Will you all go away and not take of the water of life? Come, soul - is there not one at least that God shall give to me this day for my hire - not one? May I not take you by the hand, poor, sinning, erring brother? Come, brother, let us go together and drink ...."

He then repeated the verse, "Just as I am without one plea," and continued, "As my Master is true and faithful he cannot cast away one soul that comes through, for 'him that comes through unto me I will in no wise cast out.' O spirit, now draw reluctant hearts, and give timid souls courage to believe for Jesus' sake."

You may not be able to use Spurgeon's language, but surely you can share the spirit of his conclusions. Do not be afraid of using direct, personal appeal.

(c) Practical application

Practical application is an ending closely allied to that of personal appeal. It points out the bearing of the truth upon the lives of the hearers, and seeks action.

This was the way of Jesus. "Therefore everyone who hears these words of mine and puts them into practice ... (Matthew 7 v.24); or the conclusion of the story of the Good Samaritan, "Go and do likewise." (Luke 10 v.37).

This was also the way of St. Paul. Read again chapter 15 of his first letter to the Corinthians. See how he preaches the resurrection with imagination, fire and eloquence, almost sweeping his readers off their feet, and then, in the last verse, bringing them down to earth again to face everyday realities: "Therefore, my dear brothers and sisters, stand firm. Let nothing move you. Always give yourselves fully to the work of the Lord." (1 Corinthians 15 v.58).

Some time ago I was conducting the annual enrolment service of the Boys Brigade Company. They themselves had chosen the hymns, and the one before the sermon was: "I'm not ashamed to own my Lord." I chose my text to suit the hymn: "For I am not ashamed of the gospel, because it is the power of God that brings salvation to everyone who believes." (Romans 1 v.16). Here was my conclusion: "To the ancient world, in need of life and liberty, the Gospel came. It was brought by a man who was ashamed of so much, even in his own life. But he was not ashamed of this good news. He was not ashamed because it spoke of power and salvation for everybody. There is so much in our own world, in our own country, in our own city, in our own lives, of which we should be ashamed. But we are not ashamed of the Gospel of Christ. I was glad you chose this hymn; I was glad to hear you sing it; now go out and live it."

(d) Illustrations

Some of the methods of introducing a sermon can be equally effective in concluding one. Take the use of illustration. I once preached a sermon on, "But when he saw the wind, he was afraid and, beginning to sink, cried out, 'Lord, save me!'" (Matthew 14 v.30). The conclusion was: "Christ is ever near to help when we call." Others may be near to us in danger and yet so pre-occupied that they might as well be a hundred miles away. One day I sat on a beach while a child drowned not very far away from the crowds on the shore - just out of his own depth. There were people within less than twenty yards of him, but they were all busy with their own concerns. Some were knitting; others, like myself, were reading; others sleeping; and others playing games. And the boy perished.

That can happen in spiritual life. People may be near the needy and yet be too pre-occupied to render assistance. The minister busy with his sermon; the church officers engrossed with matters of finance; others engaged with their own work or enjoyment … but Christ is always near.

(e) Quotations

Taken from poetry or hymns, quotations can also be used effectively. Speaking of the obedience of Peter in the account of the miraculous drought of fishes my conclusion was the text, an illustration, and a quotation.

Peter obeys Christ's command: "Because you say so, I will let down the nets." (Luke 5 v.5).   How we hesitate and question and doubt when all that is needed is obedience! Said the mother of Jesus on one occasion, "Do whatever he tells you." (John 2 v.5).   That is the secret.   That is how Peter's failure was turned into success.

> *Trust and obey*
> *For there's no other way ...*

In a sermon entitled "Peter correcting Christ" (Matthew 16 v.22), I again ended with an illustration and a quotation.

"It is said of Procrustean, the fabulous robber of Attica, that he made his victims fit his couch. If they were too short he stretched them out.   If they were too long he mutilated them until they fitted exactly. Is that what we try to do with God? We forget the teaching of Jesus - or rather, we try to correct it. We cannot believe that God is as Jesus revealed Him.   We narrow Him down until he fits into our own petty creeds and doctrines, forgetting that:

> *The love of God is broader*
> *Than the measures of man's mind;*
> *And the heart of the Eternal*
> *Is most wonderfully kind.*

Another way of finishing a sermon is to use the words of the text. Let this sum up all that has been said in the sermon. If you have really been keeping to your theme and topic, the text should come just as naturally at the end as at the beginning of the sermon.

A sense of completeness

Having given due regard to the importance of an adequate and satisfying conclusion, you must take care not to overdo it. There was a word - peroration - which was in great vogue at one time. The word is now seldom used. But if the word has died out, what it stood for is taking longer to die - and yet it ought to die.

Peroration means the concluding part or winding up of an oration. These perorations, so loved by older preachers, were apt to be elaborate, rhetorical and florid. They often gave the impression of artificiality and insincerity. It was as if the preacher had wound himself up, with excited voice and increased gestures, to finish with a flourish.

A sermon is not an oration. A worked-up conclusion spoils, rather than heightens, the effect of a sermon. If a man is really moved emotionally, then let him speak as he is moved. But let such a conclusion come from the sincerity of the heart. Let it be the high point to which the sermon has moved him and his congregation. The emotion must be something which has grown out of the sermon, and not something tacked on.

There are many ways of concluding a sermon. As I have already indicated, your endings must be satisfying, convincing, giving a sense of fullness and completeness to the sermon. An ideal conclusion would give the congregation the sense that anything less would have been too little, and anything more would have been too much.

Chapter 5 : The Necessity of Illustrations

The mind does not easily grasp abstract ideas. An idea, even to the more cultivated minds, becomes more vivid and interesting when presented in some concrete example.

Perhaps you are preaching on courage. If you want people to understand it, remind them of the story of Shadrach, Meshach, and Abednego. Read their answer to Nebuchadnezzar: "If we are thrown into the blazing furnace, the God we serve is able to deliver us from it, and He will deliver us from Your Majesty's hand. But even if He does not, … " (Daniel 3 vv.17-18). Or paint a word picture of Peter and John before the Jewish Council, declaring, in spite of threats, "We cannot help speaking about what we have seen and heard." (Acts 4 v.20).

The teaching of Jesus is full of concrete examples to express ideas. "Who is my neighbour?" asked the lawyer. (Luke 10 v.29). The answer could have been an exposition of the social implications of the Law. Instead, Jesus told the story of the Good Samaritan.

Illustrations help to bring into sharp focus the truths the preacher would proclaim. No true preacher can afford to neglect this art. Your congregation may be puzzled by your arguments, or by a simple declaration of the truth; but light up what you say by the use of an illustration, and they exclaim, "Now I see!"

There is a proverb which says, "He is the best speaker who can turn the ear into an eye." Truth presented by way of illustration will often open the door of many a mind which would remain closed to abstractions.

The function of illustrations

Some of the functions of illustration have already been touched upon - to simplify the truth that it may be grasped more easily; to make your sermons clearer; to quicken attention and retain interest; to make the sermon impressive, practical and persuasive; and in all these ways to be able to present the Gospel vividly and compellingly. Let me enumerate in a few short sentences the purpose and aim of illustrations.

(1) Illustrations clarify

They are like windows which let in a flood of light upon the hard mass of the sermon. They help folk to see; they give understanding; they make obscure matter clear; they make things plain.

(2) Illustrations vivify

They bring to life what you are saying. They increase the effectiveness and make the truth more impressive. Who can really understand anything about love, beauty, sacrifice, honour, without examples of these qualities in action?

(3) Illustrations beautify

See how a well chosen ornament can enhance the beauty of a woman. A diamond freshly excavated from the earth can look like nothing more exciting than a piece of glass. Cut it, polish it, and it will sparkle with light and loveliness that dazzles. As the pearl necklace which adorns the lady's throat, as the diamond cut and polished, so the illustration in the sermon enhances and beautifies.

(4) **Illustrations verify**

By this I mean that the truth you are proclaiming is tested, demonstrated, put to the touchstone, made obvious by the use of illustration.   In the time of famine there was corn in Egypt. Jacob sent his sons to Egypt for corn. After their second journey they returned with the news that Joseph was alive, and had sent for his father. But Jacob could not believe. They had deceived him before. He wanted to believe, but he was suspicious and distrustful. Their words, though true, meant nothing. Then one of the sons made him come and see the wagons which Joseph had sent full of gifts for his father. "Jacob was stunned; he did not believe them ... but ... when he saw the carts Joseph had sent ... the spirit of their father Jacob revived. 'My son Joseph is still alive. I will go and see him before I die.'" (Genesis 45 vv.27-28). Illustrations put your preaching to the proof.

(5) **Illustrations diversify**

Illustrations give a sense of variety. This lightens up the sermon which can often be heavy and stodgy.   There must be repetition in a sermon, otherwise the point you are making will never be driven home. Hearers never hear every word that is spoken.   The acoustic properties of the building may be imperfect; the listener's hearing may not be good; minds will slip back to office or home problems; weather conditions may induce drowsiness .... There are a hundred reasons - apart from the preacher - for the gap between speaking and hearing.

The preacher must keep on saying the same thing over and over again in order to make sure the congregation hears the message. "Judicious repetition" is the important phrase. But it has to be judicious. Just plain repetition makes for boredom. It is here that the use of an illustration will enable you to say the same thing without any sense of tedium and weariness.

(6) Illustrations dignify

Illustrations can lift the sermon up to higher levels. They add a touch of splendour. See how Paul elevated an appeal for Christian giving when writing to the church at Corinth. He wants them to take up a collection for the poor Christians at Jerusalem. To add weight to his appeal he uses an illustration. He tells them of the churches at Macedonia, who, out of their poverty and persecution, astonished him with gifts they had given. "They exceeded our expectations: They gave themselves first of all to the Lord, and then by the will of God also to us." (2 Corinthians 8 v.5). The appeal becomes no mere begging letter, but an opportunity of showing unity and dedication through their gifts.

(7) Illustrations satisfy

They satisfy because they clarify, vivify, beautify, verify, diversify, and dignify. These qualities of beauty, truth, lucidity, variety, and life are what people look for in a sermon. They ease the congregation. They make sermons more interesting, and make them easily remembered. Ask any member of the congregation and you will discover that illustrations are a psychological necessity.

The example of Jesus

The method of Jesus must surely be an example for the preacher. Jesus always taught in concrete rather than in abstract terms. He used as illustrations the things people were familiar with. Look at His teaching and see how much of it is given in parables and figures of speech.

Jesus did not tell us in so many words that selfishness spoils life, and brings suffering to ourselves and others. But He showed in the story of the Prodigal Son what happened to a man who lived for himself. (Luke 15 vv.11-32).

Jesus did not preach a sermon on being prepared for life's emergencies enforced with awful warnings about being unprepared. He simply told the story of the wise and foolish virgins. (Matthew 25 vv.1-13).

Again, in speaking of the difficulties and disappointments He must have experienced in proclaiming God's Word, (a parable especially appropriate for preachers), He painted a word picture of a sower going forth to sow. The sower did his job faithfully. The seed was good, but seventy-five per cent of his effort and seed were wasted. Only that which fell upon good ground was fruitful. (Matthew 13 vv.1-9).

Notice His use of similes. How often He used the phase "The Kingdom of heaven is like ..." - good seed; a grain of mustard seed; leaven; hidden treasure; a pearl of great price; a fishing net. (Matthew 13)

Look at His use of metaphors: "I am the light of the world." (John 8 v.12). "I am the bread of life." (John 6 v.48). "I am the vine; you are the branches." (John 15 v.5). "I am the good shepherd." (John 10 v.14). "I am the way and the truth and the life." (John 14 v.6). All these when speaking of Himself.

"Salt for the whole human race." (Matthew 5 v.13). "Light for the whole world." (Matthew 5 v.14). These when speaking of His disciples.

He spoke of children's games; of lilies of the field; of birds of the air; of baking bread; of bearing burdens; of laying foundations; of wedding feasts ....

Metaphors, similes, word pictures, parables, ... this was the way of Jesus. No wonder the common people heard Him gladly.

Sources of illustrations

Reading and observation are needed to build up an adequate store. Sermons must deal with the whole of living. You need to range far and wide for your illustrations. A great deal will depend upon the wideness and richness of your own lives. Those spare hours given to the study of philosophers; incidents from your holidays; your knowledge of the physical sciences; your taste in music, literature and poetry; ... all mines of illustrations. Everyday incidents; news reports; general reading; the Bible; biography; history; ... these, plus keen observation of human nature and experience, can ensure that a preacher need never be devoid of appropriate illustrations.

Perhaps you are trying to point out that there is a danger in a person's best points. An upright, honest, truthful person is to be admired, yet sometimes that integrity makes people hard, narrow, unsympathetic and harsh. Read what Jesus had to say about the self-righteous Pharisees.

In this connection Shakespeare's "Hamlet" may come back to your minds. Polonius set out to make himself agreeable.

A commendable purpose. But his endeavour to be agreeable and friendly led to losing the courage of his own convictions. Here is his conversation with Hamlet.

HAMLET: Do you see yonder cloud that's almost in shape of a camel?

POLONIUS: By the mass, and 'tis like a camel, indeed.

HAMLET: Methinks it is like a weasel.

POLONIUS: It is backed like a weasel.

HAMLET: Or like a whale?

POLONIUS: Very like a whale.

Well, clouds do assume curious shapes. It is possible for one to look like a camel or a weasel or a whale - but not all three different shapes at the same time. It is well to be agreeable and pleasing to others, but not at the expense of conviction. It is good to be popular and sociable, but not at the expense of a weakened moral character. Moral integrity is to be admired, but beware lest it leads to a lack of sympathy and hard-heartedness.

Of all the sources of illustrations, my own propensity is to find them in the Scriptures. I would make a special plea for the use of the Bible for this purpose. The Bible is full of real life, dramatic situations. The characters concerned are not mechanical, artificial, lifeless puppets, but men and women despairing, hoping, sinning, struggling, conquering … men and women pictured in all their humanity.

Here is David, the hero king, dogged by his moral weaknesses (2 Samuel 11). Samson, whose pride in his great strength was his frailty (Judges 16 vv.6-21). Hagar in distress as she is cast forth with her child at the bidding of a jealous woman (Genesis 16 vv.1-6). Ruth, whose self sacrificing love for her husband's mother has become an emblem of fidelity (Ruth 1 vv.8-17). Jephthah, with the horror of his heart expressed in his face as the sight of his daughter, joyfully running to meet him, reminds him of his rash vow (Judges 11 vv.30-36). Impetuous Peter, proudly boasting of his loyalty, yet flinching before the accusation of a serving maid (Matthew 26 vv.31-35; 69-75). John, banished to a lonely, inhospitable island, overcoming his afflictions, and sending matchless words of encouragement and comfort to his friends (Revelation 1-3).

So one could go on - indefinitely. These are mere samples of the inexhaustible stores contained in the Bible.

Sometimes a simple description can be used as an illustration. For example, Spurgeon, on a country ramble, sat down for a moment near a rustic church.

"As I sat there I moralised on the various paths which led up to the church porch. Each pathway through the grass came from a different quarter, but all led up to one point …. Even thus men come to Christ from all quarters of the compass."

Then he described the paths which brought the congregation to the church. There was the path which rose from the valley. Worshippers left the public road, crossed the brook, and ascended the hill. So each person comes to Christ from the deep places of self-abasement. They rise at every step they take.

One path came down through the churchyard, and everyone who used that path came downwards to the church. There are many who have to descend from self exaltation to find the Christ. Like John the Baptist they must say, "I must become less." (John 3 v.30).

There was a third path which came through a thick tangled wood in which there were many boggy places. Many a seeker has found his way to Jesus along the path of difficulty and affliction.

A fourth path led through a farmer's fields, from the place of toil and busyness.

So Spurgeon, by simple description, showed his congregation the paths which brought men to that little rustic church - and to Christ - in an illustration which was unforgettable.

When you are using illustrations, you are saying, "Look!" But illustrations must be used carefully. They must not be dragged in for their own sake. They are used to show thought in action. Illustrations must be clear to give lucidity; they must be accurate, especially when dealing with factual examples. Most of all, they must be relevant.

Chapter 6 : The Day of Delivery

It is for this day - the day for preaching the sermon - that you have been making all your preparation. It is at this point that you have now arrived.

There is a story of an evangelist working among the bricklayers and farm labourers of Cambridgeshire, who came to London with one of his congregation for a holiday. On the Sunday morning they went to the City Temple. When the service was over the evangelist said, "Well, Sam, what did you think of the preacher?"

"I'll tell you what it is," came the reply. "That's the sort of preaching we wants up on the Heath."

"Is it, Sam?" asked the evangelist, somewhat astonished.

"Yes," came the answer. "What we wants there is a man who has got something to say, and who knows how to say it."

How are you going to say it?

There are four ways of delivering a sermon. It could be read; delivered from memory; delivered from notes; or delivered extemporaneously, without manuscript or notes.

(a) From memory

Only once have I tried to preach by memorising. It was not a happy experience. Whether or not the congregation noticed I do not know, but I felt a sense of artificiality and unreality.

Preaching from memory has neither the advantages of the read or the spoken sermon. It puts a strain on the nerves. The mind is not free. A lapse of memory throws you off balance. You become so taken up with remembering the words that all the real sense of preaching has gone.

This is a type of delivery to be avoided, and I mention it because it is so easy to get into the habit of memorising unconsciously.

At the beginning of my ministry I used to write my sermons, read them through half a dozen times to familiarise myself with them, and then preach without manuscript.

I was not consciously trying to memorise. But one evening, my landlady found a written sermon on my desk after I had left for the service, brought it with her, and followed it as I preached.

She told me afterwards that I had repeated the sermon almost word for word, but that I grew hesitant as though I were groping for some words that I had forgotten.

I could see the danger of drifting into preaching from memory. Writing my sermon and reading it over made me concentrate too much on words. I stopped writing out my sermons from that time.

(b) Written and read

There are many who feel that sermons should always be written out, whether read or not read. One advantage of writing out the sermon is that it can curtail undue verbosity - the preacher will know when to stop! Another advantage is that much anxiety of mind is spared. There is your written sermon. All you have to do is read it. There is no fear of forgetfulness.

There is no mental strain. You do not have to go floundering and stumbling after words to express your thoughts. And you do not have to regret saying what you did not mean to say. You speak with assurance and deliberation.

On the other hand, a delivery that is too formal and faultless can do much to lose the attention of the congregation.

There is an unseen chord which links the speaker and the congregation in contact. This meeting of minds is fostered, not only by the words spoken, but by the light of the eyes, by facial expressions, by a sense of liveliness in the preacher which a read delivery often sacrifices. The contact is broken. How many times has the complaint been heard, "He never took his eyes off his notes." ?

Not everyone can read well. Monotonous, dull reading makes for loss of effectiveness, especially in times of challenge and appeal.

Another disadvantage of being dependent upon a manuscript is that you are unable to adapt yourself to circumstances. For example, once I was visiting another church where, although there were adults present, most of the children stayed in for the whole service. I was thankful that I was not tied to a manuscript. If I had been, I would have been unable to adapt myself to the needs of this younger congregation. They would have been bored by my prepared sermon, and I would have missed a real opportunity.

However, having weighed up the advantages and disadvantages, one cannot condemn this method of delivery.

Indeed, many famous preachers have found it an effective method.

(c) Preaching from notes

There are two ways of preparing notes. One way is to write your sermon out fully and then reduce it to an outline, giving the headings, key words and phrases. The other is to prepare your sermon mentally, making an outline and using this outline as your notes.

Whichever way you prepare, preaching from notes gives you spontaneity and freedom. You are able to look the congregation in the face and catch the magnetism of their eyes. You become more open to unspoken suggestions from the congregation, and will be able to respond more freely and sympathetically towards them.

You will have the sense of preaching *to* people, and not merely reciting *before* them. You will gain a sense of liveliness and vitality. You will be able to tell whether or not the congregation is accepting your message or following your argument.

In my early days I preached from notes, preparing just the outline. Knowing what I wanted to say, I left the way in which I was to say it until I was preaching. I found by experience that the right words presented themselves at the right moment.

After the first ten years, while I always prepared my sermons in note form, I always preached without the notes. Every preacher must have their own method, but for me, the best way is to have my thoughts so well ordered that I can speak freely out of a full mind. I like to fill myself with my topic; gain a firm grip on the line of treatment; see the sermon in my mind from beginning to end; and go into the pulpit knowing that I am going to say this, and this, and finish with this. I concentrate on the matter, and not the words.

(d) Extemporaneous preaching

Extemporaneous preaching means preaching without a manuscript - speaking on the spur of the moment. There are two interpretations of the word.

The strict meaning of the term means preaching without any preparation. Having a topic, standing up, and speaking upon it. Thinking on your legs.

The second, and more generally accepted interpretation, means that the topic itself has been prepared, but that the words and phrases have been left to the inspiration of the moment of speaking. This refers not to the *matter* of the sermon but to the *manner* in which it is preached.

This does not mean that this type of preparation is any easier than that of fully writing the sermon out. You save yourself the labour of writing the sermon word by word, but the thought, the study, the thinking out of the ideas, the shaping of the sermon will demand your utmost application. The sermon must be mentally absorbed. It must become part of you. You know your topic; you know your theme; you have arranged the matter in the clearest manner; all that remains at the moment of preaching is to find the words.

How to speak without notes

It was William Pitt who said, "If you are thinking of words you will have no ideas; but if you have ideas, words will come by themselves."

It is important to train your memory. You must develop the power to recall ideas and thoughts which you have prepared. These must be impressed upon your mind.

One way of improving this quality is to give the memory plenty to do. This was the method I used in my earlier days. I read a piece of literature - a short book, a chapter from the Bible, a play, a poem, or a column from a newspaper. Then I put the reading away and made a mental survey of what I had read. Sometimes I spoke the survey, carefully talking out the ideas to an unseen audience. I attempted to keep the same progressive order of the original reading. This "speaking the survey" can be a real help to the preacher.

Suppose you try this. Read, for instance, the first chapter of Genesis. Put your Bible away, and then tell an imaginary audience all about it, keeping, if possible, the sequence of ideas.

God created the heaven and the earth; God gave light; God separated the darkness from the light, giving night and day; God then created the firmament of the heaven; then came the separation of water from the land (sea and earth); the earth was made fruitful; then came the creation of the sun, moon, and stars; then the creation of living creatures (fish, fowl, and beasts); the creation of man (male and female); man given power over all living things; man received God's blessing; God was satisfied.

I suggested this chapter because you should be fairly familiar with it. But unless you knew it very well you would still find it a little difficult to keep to the correct sequence. Continue trying this exercise with unfamiliar passages and you will find an increasing power of grasping and retaining ideas.

Another quality you need to develop is mental vision. You must see the ideas with the mind. For this you must use words. The use of words for mental vision does not contradict with what I have already said about preaching sermons from memory. The words I mention now are not the words you shall speak, but the words which define and give shape to the ideas.

You cannot think without words. So, in preparing to speak without notes make an outline of the ideas you want to express. Making the outline, and familiarising yourself with it, will help to impress the ideas upon your mind and give you a deeper understanding of the topic. Let the outline be logical and progressive. This will help you to keep the continuity in the train of thought, enabling you to move naturally from one idea to the next.

Sometimes arbitrary associations, linguistic or otherwise, can be used to recollect prepared ideas. This can be done by using the letters of the alphabet. You can use the same initial letter for a series of ideas which bring the ideas back to mind quickly and easily.

Here is an example using the letter 'R'. I used this for a sermon on "See how the flowers of the field grow."
(Matthew 6 v.28).

R: Reminder.   Life is not wholly material.   The function of flowers in hospitals, sick rooms, churches, are a reminder of this.   They add a splash of colour to life.   They minister to the soul.   Man shall not live by bread alone.   We need beauty as well as bread.   We need to be reminded of that.

Rebuke.   The text is a rebuke to our over-anxiety.   This is what Jesus was talking about.   Be not over-anxious.   Such anxiety is futile and not fair to God.   It hints that we do not trust God to do His part.

Re-assurance.   The text is one that re-assures us that God cares.   "If that is how God clothes the grass of the field, which is here today and tomorrow is thrown into the fire, will he not much more clothe you?" (Matthew 6 v.30).

Recapitulation.   We need this reminder, this rebuke, this re-assurance.   This is the message the flowers give.   You can crush the wild flowers in your hands, but you cannot crush their message.

Sometimes you can use several letters in alphabetical order.   Here is an outline based on John 20 vv.19-20.   The sermon was entitled *"The Saviour's Easter Greeting"*.

B: Barriers. ("Behind locked doors.")

Bodily fear. The doors were shut because the disciples were afraid of the fury of the Jews.

Bewilderment.   The disciples suffered from mental as well as bodily fear. There was mental upheaval. They had been charged with stealing the body of Jesus. They knew they were innocent … but where was the body?

Barriers raised unwittingly. The doors were locked to keep out the Jews. So they were shut when Jesus came. Do we raise barriers against Christ when we shut out new ideas etc.?

But … He broke through ("Jesus came …"). He breaks through all barriers to reach people's hearts.

The sermon continues using the letters 'C' and 'D'.

C: Comfort. ("Peace be with you.")

Casual greeting. Used by Orientals as we use the greeting, "Good Morning."

Connect with John 14 v.27. "Peace I leave with you." A reminder of His last words to them before the crucifixion. The greeting now has more significance.

Conveys comfort … confidence … courage.

D: Demonstration. ("He showed them His hands …")

Deed, plus the word. Here was living proof - hands that had fed multitudes; blessed children; healed the sick; been nailed to the cross.

David Livingstone (illustration). In 1844 Livingstone was working in the village of Mabotsa in present-day South Africa, when lions attacked and killed a woman from the village. Livingstone shot one of the lions, which then attacked him, badly injuring his left arm before it dropped dead. His body was recognised when natives brought it back to this country by a scar on the arm which had been seized by the lion.

Declaration of victory. Victory over sin and death. "I have overcome the world." (John 16 v.33).

To preach such a sermon without notes, all you have to do is to have a mental picture of the words beginning with the initial letters ... the words printed in bold type.

Alternatively, using the same sermon as above, you could use the word that lies at the heart of the topic, and use that word as the initial letters in your outline. The central word in the title is **EASTER**. The letters can be used thus:

E: Easter evening. End of tragic day.
Environment. Upper room. Locked doors.
Extremity of disciples. Bodily and mental fear.
Entrance of Jesus.

A: Avoiding enemies. Reason for shut doors.
Automatically shutting out Christ.
Acknowledge our own barriers unwittingly raised.

S: Straight through. No barriers can keep Him away.
Submission not compulsion. Only the unwilling heart can keep Him out.
Similarly with us. No barriers except ourselves can stop Him.

T: Tells them the message, "Peace ..."
Typical Oriental message.
Tremendous meaning for them.
Takes mind back to John 14 v.27.
Theme for troubled days ahead.

E: Effect of message.
Ease of tension.
Encouragement for future.
Elation. "The disciples were filled with joy." (v.20).

R: Ratification of words. Showed hands. Proof.

Recall the story of David Livingstone (the scar).

Realisation of His claim: "I have defeated the world."

If you are mentally and spiritually prepared, if your thoughts are well ordered, if you are really full of your theme, the word **E-A-S-T-E-R** will be sufficient for your preaching. Either of the above outlines should enable you to preach the sermon quite freely.

The curse of self-consciousness

There are many to whom I have spoken about extemporaneous preaching who have wished they could preach without notes, but declare they are too nervous to attempt it. But their real trouble is not nervousness, but self-consciousness. Of course preachers are nervous. Preaching demands a lot of nervous energy. Nervousness is a condition of success. When you begin preaching there is usually an excess of nervousness, but with experience you learn to control it. This sense of nervousness must always be there if preaching is to have any vitality. It is said that even Martin Luther felt his knees knock together as he ascended the steps of his pulpit.

But self-consciousness is a very different thing. It is a subtle form of pride. It comes because a man is straining after an effect, or because he is afraid of failing and making a fool of himself. The trouble lies in the fact that a self-conscious preacher is thinking of himself rather than of his message. It is this which fills him with paralysing fear. Even Spurgeon initially suffered from this curse. He has confessed that when he made his first public speech he worried for weeks beforehand.

He began to wish that something would happen, such as breaking a leg, before the fateful occasion. The result was that when he entered the pulpit worry and tension had him so much in their grip that he made a very poor showing. He made the discovery that his trouble was self-centredness. "I had been magnifying a personal problem into a world-shaking disaster." When he saw what was causing the tension, he discovered freedom in preaching.

Effectual preaching

You have prepared yourself. You have prepared your sermon. You have decided what to say. You have decided how you are going to say it. With confidence and humility you approach the pulpit. With confidence, because, in spite of your nervousness, you know that God has called you, and God will use you.

With humility, because all your usefulness is of God. You cease to think of yourself. You take no pride in your learning or your gifts. You simply give yourself to God and ask Him to use you. Let your humility keep you simple. Simplicity of language helps to keep you relevant. Here you follow the Master. Jesus used the language of the highways and byways - the language of the people.

Relevance of language. Relevance of ideas. Relevance of illustrations. These can lead to the deepest relevance of all - the relevance of the Gospel to the deepest needs of humanity. This is your business - to help others realise this relevance.

With all this, let your preaching be positive. You are not in the pulpit to give good advice, nor merely to set good examples. You are there to declare the Good News. "God so loved the world …" (John 3 v.16). You speak of Jesus whom "God raised … from the dead." (Acts 10 v.40). This was the preaching of the New Testament. There was boldness, assurance, certainty about early Church preaching. "Now Lord … enable your servants to speak your word with great boldness." (Acts 4 v.29).

With boldness and certainty be enthusiastic in your preaching. No-one can read the preaching of Peter and Paul without being caught up in the spirit of enthusiasm with which they did their work. "We cannot help speaking about what we have seen and heard." (Acts 4 v. 20).

So, with simplicity and relevance, positiveness and enthusiasm, confidence and humility, may you give yourselves to the Privilege of Preaching. Let this prayer be in your hearts - it has long been in mine:

> *My talents, gifts and graces, Lord,*
> *Into your blessed hands receive;*
> *And let me live to preach your Word;*
> *And let me to your glory live;*
> *My every sacred moment spend*
> *In publishing the sinners' Friend.*

(verse 3 of Charles Wesley's hymn "Give me the faith which can remove …").

The carved pulpit of Caen stone at
Gloucester Street Congregational Church, Weymouth

PART THREE :
Meditations & Sermons

Included here are a number of manuscripts by the Revd. Gay which were discovered after his death.

Initially there are six meditations entitled *"Breakfast for the Mind"*, delivered on the BBC Radio 4 programme *"Lift up your Hearts"* at 7:50 a.m. each morning for a week in November 1963. The Biblical quotations in these meditations have all been taken from the Authorised Version, and not from NIV.

Following these are a collection of seven sermons.

"Breakfast for the Mind"

Monday : THE DAY IS YOURS

I wonder what you are having for breakfast? Cereals? Bacon and eggs? Toast and marmalade?

No doubt you have what you think suits you. Whatever it is, it's healthy, nourishing food, for I'm sure you believe in - what my mother used to call - "starting the day well".

The point is, we need more than eggs and bacon to put us right for the day. To make a really good start we need a *'Breakfast for the mind'*. Some big, healthy, nourishing thought that will strengthen the mind as food strengthens the body. Such a thought, assimilated by the mind, as breakfast is assimilated by the body, becomes part of us, and helps to fit us to meet the coming day.

I wonder what sort of day it's going to be for you?

Some young man may be going to his mother's funeral, today .... Some mother may be taking her child to hospital, today - almost afraid to hear the specialist's verdict. There were two actual cases like that the day I prepared this talk. That son ... mother... may not be you, of course. Such sorrow ... such fear ... may not touch you, today. But life is pretty much the same for us all. It's mostly a mixture of sunshine and shadow. No one really escapes its disappointments, worries, problems, fears .... Whatever comes, we have to face it.

But how ...?

That's the thing that really matters. And that's where this *'Breakfast for the Mind'* comes in - that big, healthy, nourishing thought. It will tone us up for the day. It will set us right to face whatever life brings with a brave heart and a quiet mind.

This week I want you to share my mental and spiritual breakfasts each day. For this purpose there's no better book than the Bible. It's overflowing with healthy, nourishing thoughts. We shall go to it - as we would go to a well-stocked larder - each morning for our breakfast.

We begin today by getting our breakfast from verser 24 of Psalm 118:

> *"This is the day which the Lord hath made;*
> *We will rejoice and be glad in it."*

Look it up ... Psalm 118, verse 24. Read the words quietly ... repeat them aloud ... learn them by heart ... and keep this thought with you all day.

You see what the words mean? God has given you another day. This is your day ... a new day. Accept it with gladness and realise what a great gift this is. Take it with gratitude and let it kindle your imagination. This day - with all its opportunities - is yours. Rejoice and be glad in it. And don't make any qualifications in accepting it. Don't spoil it by saying, "But what about my troubles, and worries, and burdens?" Yes, I know .... We've all got our trials and worries. The hundred-and-one things we've got to do, with no time to do them; that awkward interview fixed for eleven o'clock; and Aunt Maggie's coming to tea, and she does upset the children so .... Yes, it's going to be a *tough* day.   But that's why we're having this breakfast - to make us fit to meet such things.

God has given us a new day. It may bring joy or sorrow. A mixture of both, probably. Do you think it's a *paltry* gift He's giving us?   Would you rather not have it?   Suppose God withheld His gift? … Supposing He said "I have no more days to give you"?

If you want today - if it's worth having - it's worth receiving with gratitude and rejoicing.   Let us accept today - with all it brings - as a gift from God … and be thankful.

So lift up your hearts, for *"this is the day which the Lord hath made. Let us rejoice and be glad in it."*

Tuesday : IT'S COURAGE YOU NEED

You'll have heard these lines before:

> *"Life is mostly froth and bubble,*
> *Two things stand like stone:*
> *Kindness in another's trouble,*
> *Courage in your own."*

I don't know that I agree with the *"froth and bubble"* part. Life's much more than that. But the last two lines make sense, don't you think?

> *"Kindness in another's trouble,*
> *Courage in your own."*

"Courage is the thing," said Sir James Barrie. "Courage is the thing. All goes if courage goes." Yes ... it's courage we need. Not the obvious, do-and-dare kind, but that other kind - that quiet, brave endurance, which keeps us plodding on, holding fast, refusing to be beaten. The sort of courage the late King George the Sixth talked about in one of his early Christmas Day broadcasts: "Have faith in life," he said. "Bring to it your courage ... hold fast to the spirit that refuses to admit defeat."

So we take our mental and spiritual breakfast today from the Book of Deuteronomy, chapter 31, verse 6:

"Be strong, and of a good courage."

Moses spoke these words to the people of Israel. He'd come to the end of his journey. They had to go forward, facing the difficulties and perplexities of the coming days without his leadership and guidance.

You'll find the same words in the next verse too. Moses speaking to Joshua who is to take over the leadership. How Joshua would need these words and the people! *"Be strong, and of a good courage."* Take that thought with you today. Keep on repeating the words to yourself. Let them help you face your problems, and overcome your difficulties. After all, others have done it ... so can you.

"To be familiar with great minds," so runs a quotation, "may shape some greatness in your own." That is equally true of great lives, great spirits, great hearts ... the lives, spirits and hearts of those who, with courage have held fast to "the spirit that refuses to admit defeat." The more we know of lives like these, the more we ourselves catch something of their spirit, and learn that, even though it is not in our power to avoid distressing circumstances, we *can* conquer them.

Such a man was the late Franklyn D. Roosevelt. He was endowed with a famous name, and recognised as one of the leaders of his party and nation. All signs were set fair for a brilliant career. Suddenly, he was stricken with infantile paralysis which left him paralysed from the hips down. This is the end, people thought. No more public service for him. He's finished. But he would not give up. By swimming in Warm Springs - at first with his arms only - he gradually conquered his affliction, until his legs became strong enough, aided by crutches, to bear his weight. Thus handicapped, he plunged once again into the service of his fellows.

Have you ever thrilled to the singing of the *"Hallelujah Chorus"*? Whether that was going to be composed, let alone sung, once hung teetering in the balance. Handel's health and fortune were at their lowest ebb. Paralysed down one side, and threatened with imprisonment for debt, he was tempted to give up. Then he rebounded ... stood up to life with courage ... and composed the greatest of his works - *"Messiah"*!

The poet Milton, stricken with blindness, went on writing his poetry; Beethoven was still composing, though so completely deaf, that at one performance of his work he had to be turned to face the audience to *see* the applause he could not hear; Helen Keller, blind, deaf and dumb, learned to *'hear'*, and even to *'speak'*, by placing her fingers on the lips and throat of her teacher.

Yes, it's courage we need. So today, we'll fill our minds with this sustaining and nourishing *"Breakfast for the mind"*:

"Be strong, and of a good courage."

Wednesday : HOW'S YOUR FAITH?

It's funny how some things stick in your mind. The word 'faith' always brings back to me something that happened many years ago. It was the Friday night choir practice, and the choirmaster (so I was told later by a friend in the choir) was looking through the list of hymns I had sent on in advance. Turning to the choir, he said: "We're having a dose of faith next Sunday."

A dose of faith. Well ... that's one way of looking at it ... if you treat faith as a medicine. But it's more than a medicine. It's a food! More than once in the Bible we find the words: "The just shall *live* by faith." You don't *live* by medicine. You live by *food* which nourishes the body; and faith is the food which nourishes the mind and spirit.

So for today's breakfast, we go to the Bible - our spiritual larder - and from a container labelled "St. Mark's Gospel" we take these words of Jesus. You'll find the words in Chapter 11, verse 22.

"Have faith in God."

Whether food or medicine, we must have faith to live. As I see it, faith is not specifically a religious quality, but a natural, human quality. Faith is the spirit of confident hope ... "the

substance of things hoped for, the evidence of things not seen."
(Hebrews 11 v.1). Faith is believing something which cannot
logically be proved ... believing it so utterly that we are willing
to act upon it ... and run the risk that it works.

Everyone lives by faith of some sort. Some have faith in
their stars ... some in horses and dogs. Their belief is so strong
that they risk money on it. Their confident hope may not be
justified ... their faith may be misplaced ... but it *is* faith.

We have faith every time we do a week's work .... faith
that when it is finished our employer will pay us for the work we
have done. Yes - and every time we post a letter, we have faith
that it will be delivered safely. We cannot prove that we shall
get our wages, or that the letter will reach its destination. Our
employer may abscond ... the postman may let us down. But
we take the risk. We act in faith.

So you see, the question is, not: "shall we live by faith?"
but "what faith shall we live *by*?" Jesus called men to have faith
in God. To turn from inadequate, misplaced faiths, to one that is
invigorating ... bracing ... satisfying.

Just as men risk money on horses, or dogs, or their luck,
Jesus calls men to risk their lives upon God ... to live in the
confident hope that the power behind all life is the power of
goodness, love and grace. As Studdert Kennedy expressed it,
quite bluntly, "Faith is betting your heart-strings there's a God -
and that He is good."

But how do I know God is good ... that He is Love?
Maybe you don't, yet. But go out and face life in the confident
hope that what Jesus said about God is true. It won't be easy. It

118

will take courage. But that is what faith is … not credulity, but courage … courage to go on living, believing in the goodness and love of God.

That's how you learned to swim - if you can swim. You got in and splashed about. Somebody told you what to do with your arms and legs. You believed them, and acted as though it were true … and you found the water was holding you up, and you were moving forward.

That's the way to develop faith. "Have faith in God," said Jesus. Let us take this thought with us today, and we'll find that He is holding us up, and we're moving forward. The experiment will become an experience.

Thursday : ONE AT A TIME

I wonder if you've heard the story of the parrot who was kept in a cage over the doorway of a hunting club? The club was high up in the mountains of Pennsylvania. As the guests went in and out, the old parrot, with great dignity, would speak the only words he knew: "One at a time, gentlemen, one at a time."

There came a day when the parrot escaped from his cage and wandered off into the mountains. A search was made for him. Eventually he was found - only just in time. He had blundered into a hornet's nest, and the hornets were stinging him unmercifully. There he was, shrieking at the top of his voice. "One at a time, gentlemen, one at a time."

One at a time. One *day* at a time. That's the way to live successfully and effectively. That is what Jesus meant when He said:

"Take therefore no thought for the morrow; for the morrow shall take thought for the things of itself. Sufficient unto the day is the evil thereof."

These words are in the Authorised Version of St. Matthew's Gospel, Chapter 6, verse 34. They need re-translating ... and before we take them as our thought for today's breakfast, let us find out what they really mean.

The Greek word translated 'thought' really means 'to be anxious' ... 'to be troubled with cares.' That's why the Revised Version reads: "Be not therefore *anxious* for the morrow", and the New English Bible uses the same word.

Dr. Weymouth's translation reads: "Do not be *over-anxious* about tomorrow", while Dr. Moffat translates the verse: "Do not be *troubled* about tomorrow; tomorrow will take care of itself. The day's own trouble is quite enough for the day."

This is what today's *"Breakfast for the Mind"* means. Not that we should never plan ... or prepare ... or look ahead; but that we should live one day at a time ... not be so over-anxious and worried about tomorrow that today becomes full of stress and strain.

We are apt to worry and fret, aren't we? With our work, for instance. How anxious we become because we will persist in doing it at the wrong time and in the wrong place. We try to do next week's work today. We take it home with us, instead of leaving it at the office or factory. We take it to bed with us, and wonder why we can't sleep. Sometimes we take it to Church with us, and then wonder why we find nothing in the service.

Sir William Ostler once said at a dinner given in his honour: "More than anything else, I owe whatever success I may have had, to the power of settling down to the day's work, trying to do it to the best of my ability, and letting the future take care of itself."

We worry and fret about our troubles too. Most people will have enough troubles to last them for the rest of their lives. Why do we try to pack them all into one day? One at a time. That's the way to deal with them.

There are those who try to carry three kinds of trouble at the same time ... and a heavy load they make .... No wonder men sometimes give way under the strain. Their load consists of all the troubles they ever had ... all they have now ... and all they expect to have. That's too big a burden. You can't carry all that. Forget yesterday's troubles - they're passed, anyhow. Leave tomorrow's till they come. Today's own trouble is what we must carry today ... we'll find that quite enough.

One at a time. That's our thought for today. One day's burdens ... one day's worries ... one day's duties. Do not let tomorrow's troubles make you so fretful ... over-anxious ... worried ... that today is spoiled. To live one day at a time is the secret of serenity.

Friday : BE OF GOOD CHEER

I'd been visiting an elderly member of my church.

Shaking hands with her as I left, I said: "Good-bye." At once she replied, "Don't say that. I don't like the word 'good-bye'. There's something so final about it."

"All-right, then," I said, "I'll say 'cheerio'. How'll that do?" "That's better," she said. "Much better."

As I went on my way I realised that I ought to have said, "Cheer up!"; "Don't lose heart!"; for she was passing through a troublesome time. Life was getting her down. She needed something to give her fresh heart. You know … Jesus was constantly doing this … telling people to "Cheer up" … "to take heart" … to keep up their courage.

"Be of good cheer"

were the words He used. We shall take these words for our breakfast this morning. They'll help us to get through the day.

Let's look at some of the times when Jesus used these words - *"Be of Good Cheer."*

First … in St. Matthew's Gospel, Chapter 9, verse 2. They brought to Jesus a paralysed man. His friends must have brought him, hoping that Jesus would heal him. Jesus could see that what the man needed was healing of the spirit, even more than healing of the body. So He said to him, "Son, be of good cheer, thy sins are forgiven thee."

Now we know, don't we, there are times when our greatest discouragement and depression come, not from circumstances outside us, but by something wrong within us. We have been selfish … cowardly … disloyal … dishonest with ourselves and others … a sense of unworthiness overcomes us … we feel unfit to face life.

If only we could be right within, we could tackle the things without. If it is like that with you, today, take courage … keep up your heart … be of good cheer. There is One who is able … and willing … to forgive our unworthiness, and heal our spirits.

Now look at St. Mark's Gospel. In Chapter 6 verse 50, we read of the disciples toiling in an open boat on a rough sea. With the wind against them … their Master absent … three long hours before the dawn would break … they were exhausted, lonely, fearful, despairing. Then Jesus comes to them … in an unexpected way. "Be of good cheer; it is I; be not afraid."

What those disciples needed most was His companionship. He met them, and gave it to them, in the very thing they dreaded. It could be like that for you, today. Is there anything you have to face that makes you anxious … apprehensive … yes - let's be blunt - frightens you? Is it sickness … pain … sorrow … disappointment … the fear of failure? It is along such paths that many have met Christ and known His companionship. So take courage … be of good cheer … the paths we dread are not so dreadful when He is with us.

The same words again … this time in St. John's Gospel, chapter 16, verse 33. It is thought they were spoken on the way to the Garden of Gethsemane. The parting of the ways had come. For Him, a Garden of agony … and a Cross. For them, loneliness, suffering and persecution. Their hearts were heavy, their minds bewildered. The future was full of uncertainty and fear. All seemed lost. It was just then that Jesus said; "In the world you shall have tribulation, but be of good cheer, I have overcome the world."

With these words - though at times they doubted - the disciples faced the future.

I saw an old poker-work motto once on the wall of a shabby kitchen. "Life ain't all you want, but it's all you 'ave, so 'ave it. Stick a geranium in your 'at and be 'appy."

No ... life's not all we want ... not for any of us. I'm not sure about the geranium, but I do know this: if we take these words of Jesus, which speak of forgiveness, companionship, and victory, for our spiritual breakfast, we can face whatever life brings us with uplifted hearts. So ...

"Be of good cheer."

Saturday : SAVED BY THE BIBLE

The title of today's talk comes from a newspaper report. A Bible had apparently saved an American airman's life during a raid over Germany during the war. A fragment of flak tore through his leather jacket and lodged in a steel covered Bible he wore in his breast pocket. This undoubtedly saved his life.

Following the report, one newspaper suggested that such a Bible should be supplied to every service man, to be worn in the breast pocket, to give protection in battle.

Such a suggestion, whatever its practical value, savours of credulity and superstition. It could lead to an ignorant, unreasonable belief that, because a man carries a Bible in his pocket, his life is safe.

In Psalm 119, verse 11 (NIV), the Psalmist says:

"I have hidden your word in my heart."

We have been trying to do that this week. We have gone to the Bible each day for our spiritual breakfasts. We have taken from it some word to keep in our hearts and minds. It is a good thing to carry a Bible in your pocket but ... it is far better to have the word of God in your heart.

After reading this report, I began to ask questions. Who gave him that Bible - and why? It must have been someone who loved him ... who had his welfare at heart. Someone who was thinking, not only of his physical safety, but of that inner life, which is the real life.

Was it his mother, the night before he went overseas? Was it the leader of a Bible class he belonged to? It must have been someone like that ...someone who wanted him to be reminded of home ... and those who loved him.

Whoever it was, I am certain they did not give it to him just to wear in his breast pocket. They gave it to him to read - to have something to help him in the difficult days and strange experiences he would have to face. *"I have hidden your word in my heart."* You ought to read the whole of this psalm - Psalm 119. I know it's a long one - 176 verses. But they're divided into groups of eight verses each. Read one section at a time. It's all about God's Word … what it does … the help it gives … the effect it has on life.

What sort of help would the airman get through reading his Bible? Let's look at some of the verses of this Psalm. Here's one - verse 42. *"I trust in Thy word."* Trust … faith … yes, he'd need that. He was to face experiences where life would come crashing down about his ears … dangerous, beastly, devilish experiences. He would need something to keep alive his faith. Something to trust in. Some sheet-anchor for life when the world seemed to be breaking up. Something to trust in …. We need that, too.

Then look at another verse - verse 114. *"I hope in Thy word."* "Hope is my strength," says an old French proverb. Dr. Thomas Fuller once declared: "It's hope alone that makes us willing to live." Hope - the thing that keeps us going. The airman would need that - who doesn't? We can't live without hope. We can't die without it, either.

There's another thing this airman would need, too. *Guidance.* He'd be away from his home and friends. It would be a strange, uncharted path he would be treading. Some light … some guiding star he would need in the dark places of life. He would find it - and we can find it - where the Psalmist did:

"Thy word is a lamp unto my feet, and a light unto my path."

That's verse 162.

Faith, Guidance, Hope … yes … and Inspiration, Courage, Assurance … what equipment we need to face life! It's all there - in the Bible.

So we'll continue to breakfast from this most nourishing storehouse. We'll let the Word of God dwell in us richly …

"for man shall not live by bread alone,
but by every word that proceedeth out of the mouth of God."

(Matthew 4 v.4).

Address at a Young Peoples' Service

May 2nd, 1943

Introduction

I had a most interesting experience one day last week. I spent three hours in a signal box, watching the signalman at his work and even helping a little in the work itself. I want to tell you about this experience and some of the thoughts that came to me while I was there. But I must start at the beginning. First of all, I had to get out of bed at 4.30 a.m. (that wasn't so interesting). After a scrappy breakfast I caught a train. At 5.25, after a journey of about 6 miles, I arrived at the signal box where I was to stay for three hours. It was not a very big nor important signal box. It was what was called a fourth class box and had a 40 lever frame. There are some boxes with fewer levers (for there are six classes altogether) and some with very many more. Some have a hundred lever frame and there are two men on duty all the time. Some special boxes have two men and a boy to work them. So you see, it wasn't one of the largest boxes, but it was extremely interesting for all that. If you have never been in a signal box you have missed one of the thrills of life. Most of you have played with trains, I daresay, moving them from line to line, but you have to magnify the enjoyment and thrill of that a hundred thousand times before you get anywhere near the thrill and the sense of power that comes through pulling the levers, locking the points, ringing the bells, etc. It all depends on you what the train is going to do, whether it is to stop or start, keep to the main line or be switched off to a loop line. Furthermore, there is a great sense of responsibility and importance, for hundreds of lives may depend on how you do your work.

The other man's job

One of the first thoughts that came to me was that it is surprising how little we know of other people's jobs. How separated we are from one another as far as our daily work is concerned.

Office; mill; factory; mine: apart from the particular job that we are doing ourselves, these other occupations are as foreign to us as an overseas country. We know that so-and-so does something in an office, but what he does is more than half a mystery. In a daily newspaper there may be some illustrations of some new machinery for a mill, but how it works, and what the operator in charge of it does, is largely unknown, except to those who do the work.

Most of you young people have either just started work or are hoping to start very shortly. I hope you will be interested in your work; and I hope too, that you will be interested in other people's jobs. It is well worth learning something about them and what they mean to the people who do them. It develops our sympathies and understanding. It gives us a broader outlook. There are times when you are suddenly faced with difficulties in certain industries - a bus strike for example, or trouble in the coal mines. How easy it is when these things happen, to say, "Oh, those miners. They are never satisfied. They are always striking." It is easy to pass judgements ignorantly and to show a complete lack of sympathy when we don't know and don't understand.

The "Golden Rule" of Jesus (He didn't call it golden - we do that because we realise how precious the rule is) says:

"Do unto others as you would have others do unto you." (Matthew 7 v.12).

What Jesus is doing in giving this rule is pleading for a deep and wide sympathy. That is the secret of living. The more we know of the lives and troubles, the work and worries of other people, the more we can share life with them and the easier and happier life becomes.

There is an excellent illustration of this in the Old Testament. Ezekiel, the prophet, had a vision from God that he was to go down to the captives in Babylon and preach to them. They were forgetting God, ceasing to worship Him, and were turning to idols. Ezekiel goes down and as he goes he thinks over the things he is going to say to these people. Harsh things; stinging things. He is really going to lash them for their apostasy. They won't like what he is hoping to say, but he is going to be a true prophet and rebuke them harshly for their neglect of God. He gets to them, but he doesn't say the things he meant to. The story says that he sat astonished among them for seven days. He sat where they sat, seeing their miseries, their troubles, the hardships of their life, and having shared their life he could understand why it was that they had no heart for worship and praise.

That is one of the messages I would pass on to you today - a message that came to me while I sat (or rather stood) where the signalman stood. You are growing up and beginning to face life as men and women. Face it with a deep sympathy for other people. The French have a proverb: "To know all is to forgive all." Know other people as well as you can: their work; their lives; their sorrows; their trials. It will help you to live according to the Golden Rule of Jesus.

The ever-watching eyes

The next thought that came to me was the way in which the various trains are watched every minute, and the care that is taken over their running. While the train is several stations away, the signalman is told by means of bells that the train is approaching. Then he is told again when it arrives at the previous station. All this information he passes on to the next box. Then, when it arrives and leaves his station he passes that on, and also back to let the previous box know that it has arrived safely and is away on its journey. Each time a signalman sends his message it is repeated by the receiver, and not only is this watch kept on the train, but the time every message is received or sent is booked down. I don't think that there can be half a minute without some signalmen watching for a train or sending messages about it or writing down the times the messages are sent. If a train driver should suddenly decide to stop of his own accord, it would soon be known and enquiries would be made. One was made while I was there. The train had been signalled to be approaching, but for some time it didn't turn up. The signalman phoned through to the previous box. "Arthur, where's that train?" It was explained to him that it was a long goods train heavily laden and travelling slowly. "That's all right, then." he replied. "I thought perhaps it had gone for a walk across the fields."

Not only is there all this watching, and signalling, and booking, but as the train passes each box the signalman watches it to see that the doors are closed and that the train has a tail lamp. The tail lamp tells him that the train is complete.

As I watched all this care, it amazed me to think that while I have travelled hundreds of miles by train I have never once thought of all the watchful care that has been taken. And as I thought of that, other texts came into my mind. Two came immediately: one from the Old Testament and one from the New Testament: "The eyes of the Lord are everywhere, keeping watch on the wicked and the good." (Proverbs 15 v.3), and "He cares for you." (1 Peter 5 v.7). It seemed to me that in the work of the signalmen we have a picture of God, watching over us all daily, hourly, with loving solicitous care; knowing us and what we do every moment of our lives. In our joys and sorrows, in our successes and failures; when we are obedient and when we are disobedient; watching, watching, patiently, lovingly. Have you ever thought that sometimes His watching brings Him gladness and sometimes sorrow?

The loop line

One other thing happened while I was there that made me seriously think. One train, whether it was an empty goods train or not, I cannot remember, but one train was coming along quite leisurely when a message was received that another, more important train was travelling behind it on the same line. When the message came, the signalman, by arranging various points and signals, switched the first train onto a relief line and kept it there until the second train had come and gone. He then let the first train proceed after the second train had passed. That sort of thing probably happens to passenger trains occasionally, and when it does I expect the passengers begin to wonder why they have been thus switched, and why they are being held up and not allowed to proceed with their journey. If we were a passenger in such a train I expect we would guess the reason, especially as we realise in war time that there are certain trains which must get through without being hindered, and we can see the reasonableness of such a proceeding.

But that very thing often happens to us in life, and we don't always see the reason. Then it is that we get worried and anxious, sometimes even querulous. We see the way we think we should go. There seems nothing wrong about it and yet the doors seem barred. Like the story of Peter, when Jesus was explaining to them that He would have to leave them. Peter asked, "Lord, why can't I follow you now?" (John 13 v.37). Or Paul, who wanted at one time to go to Bythinia and at another time to Rome. Each time the way was barred, and he couldn't understand it. Whether the passengers can understand or not, the signalman knows what he is doing. Whether we, in life, understand it or not, God knows what He is doing. Peter didn't realise that Jesus was going to His death, and that there was very much more work for him to do in the world before he could follow his Master. Paul didn't realise at the time, though he may have later, that he was prevented from going to Bithynia because God had other work for him to do in Macedonia, and that he was prevented from going to Rome because eventually he would get there as a prisoner, and that through his preaching in prison he could do great work for that same Master.

Dr. Gravie, my old principal, wanted to be a missionary. In every way he was fit and competent, save in health. He confessed that it worried him, when he was refused on medical grounds. He wanted to do some work for God and it seemed to him that he was being held up. So he was switched over onto a loop line and became a minister at home. Continuing his studies, he became a college professor and Principal. There, in that position, he helped to train hundreds of young men to do the work that he was prevented from doing. No doubt he would have made an excellent missionary had he been allowed to go, but I can't help feeling that the work he did in training others was far more important.

So I pass the thought on to you. As you go through life, coming now and again to closed doors, being switched over to other lines and seeing other lives pass you on the journey, if you have done all you can and made every effort, and still the way is barred, don't become worried and anxious and fretful. The Great Spirit who moves the levers which work the signals of our lives knows what He is doing. Just trust in Him. Set your life according to His signals, and ultimately you will find that all things work together for good.

Father stood by me

I am not sure that I ought to tell you the next bit, but as there are probably no railway officials in the Church I think I will risk it. The signalman let me take a hand in pulling the levers and ringing the bells, which ordered the course of the trains. Several trains I saw safely in and out of the station, for although I have told you it was a small box, it was a very busy one. In three hours there was only one short break of a quarter of an hour when there wasn't something happening. As I said, I had seen several trains safely in and out of the station when, in my eagerness, I nearly made a mistake. When a train is in a station the signalman has to alter the distant signals which the train has just passed so that another train cannot come and bump into the one that is standing. But the one immediately in front of it must not be altered of course, until the train has left the station. In my eagerness I not only altered the three that the train had just passed but was also releasing the fourth when the signalman gave a shout and had his hand on the lever in a flash. Not that anything terrible would have happened, of course, even if the signal had been released. It wouldn't have caused an accident, or anything like that. The worst that could have happened would have been that the train would have been held up in the station for a few minutes. But the point was this - the signalman, whom I may as well confess was my father, stood by me. My father stood by me.

Again a text flashed into my mind. When Paul was in difficulties, for example when he was in prison and outside the prison there were men who had sworn neither to eat nor drink until they had killed him; or when he was in a boat in a rough sea and all seemed lost; or when he was on trial for his life and all his friends had deserted him - the text that Paul used on all three occasions when telling the story afterwards was "The Lord stood by me."

Will you take that message into life also? Many times you will face new experiences; many times maybe, you will find life full of difficulties; many times it will be so easy to make mistakes; many times you will be called to adventure forth for the right and the true and the good. Sometimes these occasions may be a little frightening. It is not always easy to stand for the decent and best things of life. But take this thought with you into life - even when doing what you feel to be right looks like getting you into trouble - the Lord, your Heavenly Father is standing by, to help and watch and to strengthen.

Conclusion

I have said so much to you that probably you won't be able to remember all I have said, so may I just mention again the thoughts I would have you take into life.

(1) Learn to know all you can about your fellow men and women - their lives, work, trials and sorrows, so that you can really share their lives, understand and sympathise.

(2) Live your lives in the faith that God is a loving Father watching over you day by day with anxious solicitude, and that our actions and living can either hurt or give pleasure to His heart.

(3) Don't be too fretful and anxious if you can't have all your own way in life. Our wisdom is oftentimes folly, and God knows what is best for us, and where we can serve Him best.

(4) Always remember, in the strain and stress of life - and it will come - that God never forsakes His servants. Your Father is standing by.

Teach Your Children

A Sunday School Anniversary Sermon - Preached at
Gloucester Street Congregational Church, Weymouth

*"Only be careful, and watch yourselves closely so that you do
not forget the things your eyes have seen or let them fade from
your heart as long as you live. Teach them to your children and
to their children after them. Remember the day you stood before
the Lord your God at Horeb, ..."* (Deuteronomy 4 vv.9,10)

This text has something to say about the teaching of
children. It raises three simple yet profound questions which I
want to discuss with you.

(1) Who are we to teach?

There is a story in the New Testament which shows us
clearly the value and importance of children in the eyes of Jesus.
The disciples had been disputing as to who should be greatest in
the Kingdom of Heaven. The answer Jesus gave is significant.
We read that: "He called a little child to him, and placed the
child among them." (Matthew 18 v.2).

The Church at times has been slow in following Jesus in
this respect. In other realms of life, however, the action has been
followed and the importance of the child recognised. Men have
put the child where Jesus put him - in the midst.

This is especially true in the *home*. Awake or asleep, the
child is in the midst. Awake, all the domestic arrangements are
centred around him. Asleep, there is the quiet tap at the door
when visitors arrive, the subdued conversation, the ritual of a

peep at the sleeping child before they depart. Awake or asleep, the child is the centre of household activity.

This is also true in the *nation*. The child is the crux of all social problems. At the outbreak of the war, when preparation for the grim conflict demanded the time and strength and energies of those who governed us, the evacuation of children was not forgotten - to what was hoped would be places of safety. Even in the midst of war, some of the most intense debates in Parliament - those which aroused eager interest and ardent speeches - were concerned with the children: the Education Bill; the school-leaving-age; the teaching of religion in the schools. Then since the war, as ministers well know through the signing of innumerable forms, the child has again been prominent in the provision of family allowances.

Themistocles, that noted Athenian soldier and reformer, in his day the most influential person in Athens, is reported to have said that: "Greece governed the world; the Athenians governed Greece; he governed the Athenians; his wife governed him; and his little girl governed his wife." It was a pagan's way of testifying to the importance of the little child.

Now I do not think that I am exaggerating too much when I deduce from the words of Moses and still more from the action of Jesus that the child must have its place in the *church*.

Of course we must not sentimentalise over children. There are people who think all children are little angels. Those who think like that have never taught in a Sunday School. Quite apart from sentimentality, however, the Church must not be behind the home and the nation in recognising the value and importance of the little child.

F. W. Boreham tells a story of an old man's prayer. It was at a prayer meeting at the close of such a service as this. In the service frequent references had been made to 'the rising generation'. The old man prayed thus: "O Lord, we pray thee to bless the rising generation of which we have been hearing; for thou knowest, O Lord, there was no rising generation in our young days."

Behind the unconscious humour of that prayer was an unconscious criticism of the Church. "Teach thy children and thy children's children."

(2) What are we to Teach?

We should have to read through the whole of this chapter to discover what it is that we are to teach. Moses mentions various laws, commandments, statutes, the story of Divine help and deliverance from slavery. All this is in Deuteronomy chapter 9. But it can all be summed up in one phrase: our personal experience of God: "Remember the day you stood before the Lord your God at Horeb."

At the command of God Moses had assembled the people at Horeb. The mountain burned with fire. There was darkness all around. They saw no form, but they heard a voice - the voice of God speaking to their hearts. That moment they were sure that God was with them. It was personal experience of His presence. That is what we have to teach - the dealings of God with us - our personal experience of One who has helped us, warned us, cheered us, strengthened us, lightened our way, shared our burdens, the God we know. "Remember the day you stood before the Lord your God at Horeb."

During the last twenty years or so there has been a great improvement, outwardly at least, in regard to Sunday School methods and teaching. There was a time when almost anyone would do for a teacher, and anything they happened to say would pass for teaching. Now the situation has changed. Today the Sunday School Teacher must read one or more of the many magazines printed for their especial benefit. They must attend the Preparation Class for instruction and discussion. There must be periodic talks to teachers' groups on *"The Background of the Bible"*; *"The Elements of Teaching"*; *"Psychology and the Child"*; and so on. Let there be no mistake about it, all this is good. It is well to recognise that the best, and nothing less than the best, is good enough for the children. The importance of the Sunday School Teacher's task is such that no training or preparation should be spared which can aid the teacher in doing the job more effectively. All this must be acknowledged. It still remains true, however, that no matter how accomplished the teacher may be, unless they possesses an experience which they can share with those they teach, their teaching is in vain.

There is a great deal of truth in the saying that Christianity is not a thing to be taught, but to be caught. It is not so much what is said that counts, as the impact of the personality upon those taught. Shining through all the lessons we teach there must be our own personal knowledge of God and the faith we have in Him. Our task is not merely to relate Scripture knowledge. The Sunday School examination, however important, is not the be-all and end-all of Sunday School teaching. The importance of our work lies in training character and moulding life; in teaching the children to know and love and serve God.

I can remember even now the teacher of a boy's class in a little Welsh village church. Rough, ready, unlearned, I don't suppose he had ever read the *Sunday School Chronicle* or the *Concise Guide* in his life. Yet what a wonderful grip he had upon his class! The boys never came away without knowing something more of the meaning of the Christian life.

Use the best methods; put all you can into training and preparation; but do not forget the heart of the message. Teach the laws, the statutes, the commandments, the history, the stories … but especially "the day you stood before the Lord your God."

(3) Why are we to Teach?

The answer to this question is to be found later in this chapter: "So that it may go well with you and your children after you and that you may live long in the land the Lord your God gives you for all time." (Deuteronomy 4 v.40).

This address by Moses was given to the children of Israel just as they were about to enter into the Promised Land. For years they had been travelling through the wilderness. Now a new experience was to come to them. They are to take possession of a new land and settle there. They themselves may not live to enjoy it very long, but their children will. This teaching is to fit them for the experience of living in a new land.

At all times this is true of children. They have to face a new land with new experiences. The land of manhood and womanhood is far different from the land of childhood. New dangers, new temptations, new responsibilities, new tasks: all these will meet them as they enter the new land. That is why we are to teach - to fit them for this new land, so that when they enter it, it may be well with them.

In these days, however, this point has deeper significance still. The new land our children will enter is not only the land of adult age, but a land of entirely new conditions, owing to the upheaval that has shaken the world and its resultant aftermath.

Where is this new world that we heard so much about during the war? It was to have been far better than the old. Social conditions were to have been improved; barriers between men were to be broken down; there was to be more kindness, sympathy, understanding, fellowship. That was our Promised Land. That is the kind of world we want - for ourselves, but most of all for our children.

Will these dreams that we had of a better world ever come true? Or were they just wishful thinking? The new world may be far worse than the old unless by precept and example we fit the children for it. After all, it will be their world. Like the Jews of old we may enter the new land for a period, but it will be their world and they will have the making of it.

There will be no new world unless there are prepared for it men and women of fine ideals and splendid character. People of faith, hope and love; who believe in law and order, in brotherhood and fellowship, in helpfulness and kindness, in understanding and sympathy - in short, men and women who know and love and serve God. These men and women whom the world will so vitally need, are the girls and boys in our homes and in our schools. Theirs will be a tremendous task. That is why we are to teach, so that when they enter upon this new land, all will be well with them.

(4) Our re-dedication

We have asked our questions and answered them. Who are we to teach? - the children. What are we to teach? - our personal experience of God. Why are we to teach? - that it may be well with them in the new land. Now let me turn back to the first phrase of our text. All we have discussed so far rests upon this. "Only be careful, and watch yourselves closely."

It seems to me that Moses was a little afraid that in the upheaval and excitement of entering this new land, especially without his leadership, the people would grow forgetful of their past experiences. He was fearful lest they would allow these things to pass from their minds. The new land depended upon their children, but their children depended upon them. So he utters his warning and pleads for their self-dedication. Several times in different words, we have the warning in this chapter: "watch yourselves closely ..."; "watch yourselves very carefully ..."; "Be careful not to forget ...." (Deuteronomy 4 vv.9,15,23).

That is why we are here tonight. We have been celebrating the Anniversary of our school. It is well that with such a long and glorious history we should celebrate. But celebration is not enough. We are here, parents and teachers, that we might renew our vows, offer again our obedience and service, to ask forgiveness for our weakness and failure, and to seek God's strength to aid us in our work.

Is there any greater work on earth than the forming, fashioning, moulding the lives and characters of the little ones? Let us re-dedicate ourselves, praying that God will strengthen us and accept our service, that we may prepare our children for their new land.

"Only be careful, and watch yourselves closely so that you do not forget the things your eyes have seen or let them fade from your heart as long as you live. Teach them to your children and to their children after them. Remember the day you stood before the Lord your God at Horeb, ..."

The Prayer Life of Jesus

"But Jesus often withdrew to lonely places and prayed."

(Luke 5 v.16)

What a picture the Gospels present of the Praying Christ. Here we find One who not only urged men to pray, not only gave them a pattern prayer, but who set before men His constant example of His own prayer life. After His baptism; before calling the disciples; on the Mount of Transfiguration; in the Garden of Gethsemane; and on the Cross at Calvary, Jesus held converse with His Father.

In this sermon I want to consider six occasions on which Jesus prayed. From them we can learn how Jesus illustrated in His own life the teaching He gave the disciples: "that they should always pray and not give up." (Luke 18 v.1). In the morning and in the evening, before and after a venture, on the mount and in the valley, we find Jesus at prayer.

The beginning and the end of the day

In Mark's Gospel we read: "Very early in the morning, while it was still dark, Jesus got up, left the house and went off to a solitary place, where he prayed." (Mark 1 v.35).

The previous day had been the Sabbath. Jesus had taught in the synagogue; healed a man with an unclean spirit; healed Peter's wife's mother; and then spent the rest of the day in healing and casting out devils.

And now, before the dawning of a new day - a day which is to be spent in healing and teaching - He seeks the fellowship of His Father.

I remember, many years ago, taking part in a caravan mission. The plan of each day was much the same - reading and preparation in the morning, visiting and gathering a congregation in the afternoon, holding services and speaking in the evenings. Every morning, with all our work set out before us, we prayed together as we planned the details of the day's work.

In the morning, the whole new day is stretching out before us, unsullied and unspoiled. A day of opportunity. How are we going to use it? What are we going to do? What experiences will it bring to us? There may be joy or sorrow; success or failure; probably a mixture of experiences. If we are to face the day successfully and use it in any worthwhile way, we need to pray. The living of the Christian life is difficult enough. We should not make it more difficult by neglecting the source of power and strength.

But Jesus did not just pray in the morning, for we read in this same Gospel of the evening of another day. Again it had been a busy day. He had preached and taught. He had received the bad news of the death of John the Baptist. He had fed a great multitude, and then, "After leaving them, he went up on a mountainside to pray." (Mark 6 v.46).

Praying at the end of the day is as needful as at the beginning. After our work, our achievements, our service, our temptations, our struggles, our failures; we need to meet with

God to thank Him for victories won, and to seek His forgiveness for our slackness and failure.

Before and after a venture

In St. Luke's Gospel we read what Jesus did before the choosing of the Twelve. "Jesus went out to a mountainside to pray, and spent the night praying to God. When morning came, he called his disciples to him and chose twelve of them." (Luke 6 vv.12,13).

This was an important step in the mission of Jesus. It was something which would make a difference to Him and to those chosen. Now they were definitely linked up with Him in God's work. Now they were His responsibility. They left all and followed Him. Before such a tremendous undertaking as this, Jesus prayed.

In a similar way our choices and decisions are fraught with tremendous consequences. Our choice of friends, our lines of conduct, our day-to-day decisions are of such seriousness and significance that they demand a wisdom and guidance greater than our own.

Again we find Him praying after the return of the seventy (Luke 10 v.21). Jesus had sent them out to prepare His way. It was a responsible task that He had placed upon them. How they performed it would make things easier or harder for their Master. Now they were back, the task successfully performed. They had attempted great things for Him. They found that He had kept His promise, and they had found power and joy in their work. Full of enthusiasm they gave their report, and it is then, at the height of success, that Jesus prays.

This is the time when, as a rule, we forget to pray more than at any other time. We are driven to prayer when we have failed. When, like the men the Psalmist described (Psalm 107 v.27), we are "at our wits' end", we throw ourselves upon God. But when things have gone well with us, when we have been successful, then, too, is the time for praying.

On the mount and in the valley

There are two more contrasting occasions in which we find Jesus at prayer. The first was on the Mount of Transfiguration. "About eight days after Jesus said this, he took Peter, John and James with him and went up onto a mountain to pray. As he was praying, the appearance of his face changed, and his clothes became as bright as a flash of lightning." (Luke 9 vv.28,29).

Life is a series of ups and downs, of mountainous country and flat. Here the disciples are on the mountain top with their Master. They see Him transfigured before them. They have a glimpse of His glory. It is for them a moment of satisfying ecstasy. For their Master it is a moment of prayer.

Dr. G. Adam Smith tells of an experience he once had climbing in the Alps. Reaching the summit of a lofty peak after hours of hard climbing, the foremost guide stepped on one side so that the Doctor might be the first to plant his feet on the hard-won heights. With the labour of climbing over, and exhilarated with the thought of the wonderful view awaiting him, but forgetful of the high gale that was blowing on the other side of the rocks, Dr. Smith sprang eagerly up and stood erect to see the view. The guide hurriedly pulled him down with the exclamation, "On your knees, sir. You are not safe here except on your knees."

An exalted position, in the realm of the spiritual or the material, demands that we go on our knees.

The contrasting scene was in the Garden of Gethsemane. The exaltation was gone. No Moses or Elijah now to hold converse with Him, only a few imperfect disciples who could not understand what was happening nor enter into His suffering. A few dull souls who could not share His agony, nor even keep awake while He fought out His lonely battle. It was with His soul troubled, and in an agony of spirit that "He withdrew about a stone's throw beyond them, knelt down and prayed." (Luke 22 v.41).

It is said that a young artist came one day to William Blake, the poet, in great distress of spirit. He was passing through one of those dry periods when his inspiration had deserted him. He was in despair. After listening to him patiently the poet turned to his wife and said, "We, too, know these dry periods, these arid seasons of the soul. When they come, what do we do?" Seriously his wife answered, "Then, Mr. Blake, we kneel down and pray."

In exaltation and despair, in holy joy and bitter sorrow, on mountain top and in the valley, kneel and pray.

These incidents preach their own sermon. The fact that the Master prayed teaches us more than the words of His prayers. Here in these scenes the Lord of Life shows us our need for communion with God in all the experiences of life.

Morning and evening; before and after decisions and ventures; in joy and in sorrow; Jesus went to lonely places ... and prayed.

"A man reaps what he sows"

(Galatians 6 v.7)

You reap what you sow. What could be plainer than that? Sow potatoes, you reap potatoes. Sow cabbages, you reap cabbages. That's the law ... a logical principle ... an acknowledged, universal truth.

I remember once being shown round a friend's garden. He was proud of his garden, and rightly so. Quite a large garden it was, divided up into beds and plots in a most artistic way. But there was one part which had caused him disappointment. He had set his heart upon having a little flower garden of differing shades of blue. He sowed the seeds, but when the flowers appeared, a patch of red in one corner spoiled the effect.

"How did that happen?" I asked.

"I don't know," he said, "I thought I had planted blue flowers there, but I couldn't have, for those red ones came up. A mistake in the packing, I suppose. Wrong label on the packet, or something."

I was reminded of the parable that Jesus told about the man who planted good seed in his field, and how an enemy came and planted tares among the wheat. When the harvest came his servant was surprised to find the tares growing among the wheat. "'Sir, didn't you sow good seed in your field? Where then did the weeds come from?' 'An enemy did this,' he replied." (Matthew 13 vv.27,28).

That's the point: neither the master in the parable, nor my friend, suggested that a miracle had happened to change wheat into tares, and delphiniums into poppies. They were surprised, naturally, but they didn't suggest that Nature had suddenly gone haywire.

"A mistake … a wrong label," said my friend.

"An enemy," said the farmer.

Both would agree that if tares and poppies came up, then somehow or other tares and poppies must have been sown. For that's the principle of Nature - you reap what you sow.

The Apostle Paul applies this law of Nature to Human Nature. Sow the seeds of jealousy, envy, selfishness, hatred, bitterness - ugly, evil things - and you reap a harvest of thorns. Sow seeds of goodness, kindness, sympathy, service and love, and you reap a harvest that satisfies. Using the Apostle's own words "Whoever sows to please their flesh, from the flesh will reap destruction; whoever sows to please the Spirit, from the Spirit will reap eternal life." (Galatians 6 v.8). You reap what you sow.

Now my friend in his garden, and the farmer in the parable, not only believed this law of Nature, but they also believed something else, something which follows from this general rule - follows as a natural consequence - something which is equally true: *that no-one can break the connection between sowing and reaping.*

That's why they spoke about an 'enemy' and a 'wrong label'. That's why they looked for some other explanation for the tares and the poppies. Tares produce tares, and wheat produces wheat. And you cannot break the connection.

That's self-evident. Nothing could be more obvious. Even the meanest intelligence can realise that. There's no need to labour the point, surely!

Well now, if I were speaking of the realm of Nature only, there wouldn't be any reason to labour the point. For *there* we recognise this truth and accept it.

But there are people who just *won't* accept this truth in other spheres. They don't realise that this has something to do with the consequences of life; that what is true in the harvest field is also true in our daily living.

Let me give you an illustration.

There were once two maiden ladies who belonged to a certain church, and one day their minister called to see them. During his visit he asked them a very simple question: "What's the name of the people who've come to live next door?" He was most surprised when one of them answered: "Oh, we don't know. We never mix with people indiscriminately. Our parents instilled that into us when we were quite small children. You have to be so careful. You're never quite sure who you are mixing with."

Well the minister went away and got his information somewhere else.

But there is a touch of poetic justice about this story. There was a 'flu' epidemic, and these ladies, in common with others, became victims. It was some time before the minister heard of their illness, but eventually he called. He found them most upset. They'd been ill for two weeks and no-one from the church had called to see them. They did think *someone* might have visited them. Indeed, they were so upset that they had almost made up their minds to leave the church, *because there was no friendliness in the church.*

As he listened to them, the minister seemed to hear the echo of some other words which had been spoken in that very same room only a short while before: "Oh, we don't know ... we never mix with people ... you have to be so careful ... you're never quite sure who you are mixing with."

If you want to have friends, you've got to be friendly. It's no use living self-centred, self-contained lives, keeping yourself to yourself. It's no use sowing the seeds of estrangement and isolation, and then expecting a harvest of friendship. To reap *that* harvest you must sow the proper seeds - kindness, helpfulness, understanding, sympathy.

"A man must keep his friendships in repair," said Dr. Johnson. Emerson put it still more bluntly when he said "If you want a friend - *be* one."

You can't break the connection between sowing and reaping. The harvest in the Autumn depends upon the seed-time in the Spring. What a pity we forget that so often in our daily living!

Just one more thought. *Since, once we've sown, the reaping is beyond our changing, we need to be most careful about the sowing.*

I learned this lesson once in a most practical way. It was the first time I had a garden of my own. I sowed potatoes plentifully ... practically filled the garden with them ... but I put in very few greens. There wasn't much room left, anyhow.

When the harvest came, I had a wonderful crop of potatoes, but, naturally, very few greens. You can guess how disgusted I was when I discovered that potatoes, that year, were most plentiful and very cheap. But greens were scarce and expensive.

How I wished my garden had fewer potatoes and more greens. But it was too late. It couldn't be altered. But next year ... ah, next year ... I'd be more careful what I planted. For I had learnt my lesson.

I remember once listening to a Probation Officer speaking about Juvenile Delinquency. He told us about a 14-year-old boy who was the terror of the neighbourhood. He had been before the Juvenile Courts several times, but nothing moved him - neither appeals to his better nature, nor threats of punishment. He was just a hopeless case that no-one could do anything with.

The Probation Officer took the trouble to trace his history. He had been brought to the town twelve years before as a child of two years old. His mother brought him. She found rooms, left the child with the landlady while she went shopping (so she said), and then walked off, just disappeared and left him.

Is it surprising that with such sowing the harvest should be so tragic?

A business acquaintance once bluntly told me that he didn't believe in special days of prayer. He'd attended Church on such a day the previous Sunday, and he hadn't found any comfort or strength or satisfaction in so doing. I think he was trying to shock me. I wasn't really surprised at what he said. From what I knew of him he hadn't prayed - publicly or privately - for years. Now prayer is fellowship with God. A means through which we speak to Him and He speaks to us. If we need to keep our human friendships in repair, we need to keep our fellowship with God in repair too. How can a man sow the seeds of neglect and indifference to God for years and years, and then suddenly expect a harvest of satisfaction and comfort and strength?

No. We need to look to the sowing. And this is true not only for individuals, but in national and international life as well. You cannot sow the seeds of hate and expect love to blossom. You cannot sow the seeds of injustice and expect to reap justice. You cannot sow the seeds of selfishness, suspicion, distrust, and expect a harvest of brotherhood and peace.

How many times have you heard people say, as they have looked back over their lives regretting some foolish action, or some lost opportunity ... how many times have you heard them say, "If only I had my time over again!"

What they really mean by those words is this - that they wish they'd been more careful about the sowing, because they've discovered they couldn't alter the reaping. There may be some of you who are thinking, wistfully, "If only I *could* have my time over again, I'd ... But it's too late, now."

In one sense that is true. You can't alter the reaping of your previous sowing, any more than I could change my potatoes into greens. I'd planted potatoes, and I reaped potatoes, and that was that!

But ... you keep on sowing every year in the garden. And the following year I was a little wiser in my sowing ... more balance ... more proportion. And we keep on sowing *every day* in the harvest of life. The sowing may have been faulty in the past, but there's a new day tomorrow. Another opportunity for sowing.

Then scatter seeds of kindness, sympathy and helpfulness; of goodness, faith and fellowship. Then, for you, and for others, "Instead of the thorn-bush will grow the juniper, and instead of briers the myrtle will grow." (Isaiah 55 v.13).

To sum up: It is a law of Nature, and of Life, that we reap what we sow. Out of this springs another law - you cannot break the connection between sowing and reaping. Since the reaping, then, is beyond our changing, we need to be most careful about the sowing. For in daily life, as well as in the garden, the harvest in the Autumn depends upon the sowing in the Spring.

"Yet ..."

(Editor's note: This sermon was based on the Authorised Version translation using the word "Yet".)

"To be familiar with great lives," declares an old saying, "may shape some greatness in our own." How true that saying is!

Take, for instance, Helen Keller - blind, deaf, and dumb. Who can read of her struggle to overcome these adversities, and of the generous giving of herself to help others in their sufferings, without feeling challenged to face their own adversities more bravely?

Robert Louis Stevenson, racked with pain, wrote from his sick bed a book so cheerful in spirit that one reviewer declared that the author obviously knew nothing of pain and suffering, otherwise he could not have written such a book. Who can hear that without desiring that he, too, may learn to face life with "gallant and high-hearted happiness"? (The Happiness Prayer).

How many have been stirred to the depths as they have reflected upon the oft-told story of Captain Oates, that very gallant gentleman, who walked out into a raging blizzard to die, rather than handicap his companions and bring them to their deaths.

Yes. The more we see of greatness, read about it, live with it, the more we are inspired to achieve greatness ourselves.

The saying also holds true when we amend it a little and apply it to religion. "To be familiar with great faith may shape some greatness in our own." The experiences of our fellows help us far more than we realise. To see others holding on to their courage, their assurance, their faith, in times of trial and tribulation, inspires us to similar faith and assurance.

For that reason it will be good for us to look at the experiences and hear the words of some of those who, through bitter experiences, still trusted in God, and by His power were able to overcome. As we ponder their words and contemplate their faith and courage, we may well be inspired to face life's bitter moments with uplifted hearts and renewed strength.

Listen to these words: "Though the fig tree does not bud and there are no grapes on the vines, though the olive crop fails and the fields produce no food, though there are no sheep in the pen and no cattle in the stalls, *yet* I will rejoice in the Lord, I will be joyful in God my Saviour." (Habakkuk 3 vv.17 - 18).

Recall another example. You know the story of Job. He was a prosperous and upright man. There were those who felt that his uprightness depended upon his prosperity. There are always those who declare that it is easy to be good when life rests in pleasant places. Take Job's prosperity away; let him learn something of the hardship of life; let him experience something of the struggle of poverty; let the hand of sorrow touch him; let disaster dog his steps; then see what sort of life he lives!

He did learn. Suffering, sorrow, disaster - he faced them all. He lost his possessions, his family, his health. There came to him trouble after trouble, disaster after disaster, until we see him, everything lost, smitten with boils, derided by his wife, reproved by his friends.

What will he say to these things? Will he, as his wife was so ready to do, "Curse God and die." (Job 2 v.9). Here is his answer - an answer one feels like shouting out aloud with triumphant joy. "Though he slay me, *yet* will I hope in him" (Job 13 v.15).

Consider another illustration of this abounding faith. In Psalms 42 and 43 the Psalmist describes a time of great tribulation, a time of longings and tears. "My tears have been my food day and night." (Psalm 42 v.3). His taunting enemies deride him as one who has been forsaken by God. "Why have you forgotten me? Why must I go about mourning, oppressed by the enemy? My bones suffer mortal agony as my foes taunt me, saying to me all day long, 'Where is your God?'" (Psalm 42 vv.9,10). It is enough to suffer the bitterness of life's ways without having scornful derision adding insult to injury. No wonder the Psalmist mourns because of the oppression of his enemies. His soul pants, and thirsts, is cast down, and disquieted. Yet again and again his triumphant faith emerges. Three times in these two short Psalms we have this clarion call bidding his soul take fresh hope: "Why am I so sad? Why am I so troubled? I will put my hope in God, and once again I will praise Him, my saviour and my God." (Psalm 42 v.5; Psalm 42 v.11; Psalm 43 v.5). (The Authorised Version has: "I shall YET praise Him.")

Are you not thrilled with these words? There is something majestic about a faith like this. A man would be very dull of heart indeed if he were not moved, tingling with emotion, at such a glorious faith. "When everything goes wrong, YET will I rejoice," the prophet said. "Though he slay me, YET will I trust," declared Job. "In spite of my tears, my fainting heart, the bitter scorn of my enemies, I will YET praise Him" cried the Psalmist. It does the heart good to be familiar with such great faith.

What was this faith? What did it consist of? How was it that these men, in spite of national disaster, personal catastrophe and bitter jeering, were able to have such an amazing trust in God?

There is a threefold answer. First, they believed that life was in God's hands. They did not expect life to be always the same. There are exhilarating heights and humiliating depths in every experience. Some days are good, and some are bad. Life has its sunshine and storms, its smiles and frowns. But whatever happens, at the back of all life there is God. His hands hold the reins. So let it come, whatever it may be. God is still there, watchful and loving.

That is the picture given by Isaiah. "Can a mother forget the baby at her breast and have no compassion on the child she has borne? Though she may forget, I will not forget you!" (Isaiah 49 v.15). What a wonderful picture we have here. The prophet imagines a mother's love, the most marvellous of all human qualities. A mother's love. What things are endured and suffered by a mother. Yet even that fails sometimes. God's love never fails. (The Authorised Version has "YET will I not forget thee.") That was what they believed. Behind all life there was God, faithful and loving. No wonder they could rejoice and trust.

Then, secondly, they believed that God gives special grace for special needs. The greater the misfortune, the greater the comfort; the deeper the distress, the more infinitely tender and patient the love. That is true with a mother's love. A child will stumble and fall in his play. He begins to cry. With a loving laugh the mother will pick him up, kiss him, and say, "There, there, never mind. It's better now." And in two minutes the child is happily playing again. But a son or daughter will come home with a hurt in the heart - some disappointment, some failure, some let-down by friends, some loving friendship broken down - and again the mother will comfort. But there is no two minute business about this. For hours, if necessary, the mother will talk, comfort, soothe, encourage, till the wound is closed and the hurt is healed.

That is what these men believed about God. His loving care was like a mother's - except that it was infinitely greater. The more they needed Him, the more He gave of strength, comfort and love. The greater the need, the greater grace to meet that need. No wonder they could trust and rejoice.

Finally, believing that life was in God's hands; believing that the more they had need of Him the greater was His help; they also believed that whatever else failed, He would never fail.

Men are apt to put their trust in so many things that fail them in the end. Riches, position, health, popularity - how often have these proved to be the very weakest of crutches. How bitter the final realisation when men have placed - or rather misplaced - their faith in objects that were unworthy. But God remains faithful. So what does it matter what happens in life as long as we know that God will never fail us? What does it matter what we lose, as long as we are assured that we cannot lose God? The Psalmist said, "I was young and now I am old, YET I have never seen the righteous forsaken." (Psalm 37 v.25). He had seen them in many conditions. He had seen them in poverty, in sickness, bearing burdens, in trial and tribulation. He had seen them mocked at and scorned by men, but he had never seen them forsaken by God.

This, then, was the faith of those whose experiences we have been considering. They believed that life was in God's hands; that whatever their need, He was able to supply that need; and that whatever else failed them, He never would. With that faith in their hearts they were strong, dauntless and courageous.

To be familiar with great faith may shape some greatness in our own. May God grant that, having pondered afresh such examples of joyous, exultant belief, our own faith may be so shaped that we, too, may be inspired to face life with courage.

Faith Founded on Facts

"So that you may know the certainty
of the things you have been taught"

(Luke 1 v.4)

We live in a perplexing world - a world of uncertainty, of shifting values. Such uncertainty leads to a feeling of insecurity, and breeds indifference.

We find this indifference and laxity in almost every realm of life. Politics, for instance. Politics, in its original meaning, meant a deep and genuine concern for the well being of men. As such one would expect to find the citizens of any country politically conscious. Yet again and again, especially at election times one hears the cry, "How is it that people are not more politically conscious?" The laxity and indifference shown at these times is due to the uncertainty and perplexity regarding politics and politicians.

The same attitude is to be found in the realm of social life. When Louden, the landscape gardener, reached the age of twenty, he wrote in his note-book, "I am now twenty years of age, and perhaps, a third of my life has passed away. Yet what have I done to benefit my fellow men?" How many young people in this day and generation even bother to wonder what they have done, or can do, for their fellows? There seems to be no sense of community or vocational service, no real concern for their fellows, no social consciousness. Why? Because there is no certainty about the purpose and meaning of life. No solid foundation for living.

When we turn to religion we find the same laxity and indifference. Religion, which brings us into fellowship with God; which makes us fellow-workers with Jesus Christ; which gives zest and vitality to our living; which banishes our loneliness and gives us a power and a strength we can find nowhere else - here, surely, we will find men concerned, eager, passionate. But it must be confessed, quite frankly, that little of this is evidenced in the lives of the majority, and that religion, even in the lives of professing Christians, is often a half-hearted affair. Why this indifference, this unconcern, this listlessness? Is it because there is no real assurance, no definiteness, no certainty about the things we profess to believe?

It is with this matter of certainty in religion that Luke deals in the preface to his Gospel. In the four verses which form the 'Introduction' he makes certain explanations. First, he explains his authority for writing: "Since I myself have carefully investigated everything from the beginning." (Luke 1 v.3). He knew what he was writing about. Probably an eye-witness himself, he had taken pains to enquire deeply into the evidence of other eye-witnesses. Others had written about the life of Jesus, and he had gone over their work carefully, checking one against the other, until his mind was full, steeped in the record of the life of Jesus. That is his authority. He knew what he was writing about.

Besides explaining his authority, he explains his purpose. Others have written about the life of Jesus, but it is Luke's purpose to deal with the incidents in his Master's life chronologically, to write them down 'in order'. He plans to give a connected account, a complete story, as far as the records went, of the life of Jesus Christ.

But he has a deeper purpose still. That purpose is to make Theophilus quite sure of the things he had been taught. Theophilus may have been a definite person or, the name meaning what it does, "one who is dear to God", Luke may have used it so that it may apply to any early Christian. But whoever Theophilus was, he had already been brought into touch with the Christian faith. He had heard the Christian story from the lips of others. This Gospel was written so that he may be confirmed in the things he had learned by word of mouth. It was written to give him certainty, assurance. It was written, as Dr. Moffat puts it, "to let you know the solid truth of what you have been taught." Luke set out to give Theophilus the facts which were to be the foundation of his faith.

At the heart of Christianity there is the fact of Christ. There can be no mistake about that. There is much in Christianity which has not been derived from Christ, much, for instance, from Judaism. This is not surprising when we remember that the first Christians were Jews, and would tend to carry over something of the hardness and legalism of Judaism into their new faith. Again, it is only to be expected that during the expansion of Christianity, and its penetration into the Roman Empire, elements of the mystery religions of the Empire, and of Greek philosophy would creep in and become part of this new religion.

But, in spite of these accretions, the heart and core of the Christian Gospel is the fact of Christ - His birth; His life; His teaching; His suffering; His death; His resurrection.

Browning, in his *"Bishop Blougram's Apology"* emphasises the same truth. "What think ye of Christ, friend?" asks the Bishop, and then, almost in the same breath, "Like you this Christianity or not?" To the poet, Christ and Christianity are one.

But the truth discovered by the missionary and the poet had long before been discovered by the apostle. Perhaps one of Paul's greatest failures was his speech at Athens. There are some very fine things in that speech: he speaks of God being not very far away; of One in whom we live and move and have our being; of how, behind the creation of this world there is Providence, not chance; of the folly of worshipping idols; but the specifically Christian message is not stressed - just a passing reference to the resurrection. Although a few accepted his teaching, the majority were unmoved. He must have departed from them with a sense of failure. It was this, according to some scholars, which led him to write penitently to the Corinthians, "For I resolved to know nothing while I was with you except Jesus Christ and him crucified" (1 Corinthians 2 v.2).

But how can we have this certainty about Christ? How difficult it all seems at times. As Ray Palmer's hymn has it:

> *Jesus, these eyes have never seen*
> *That radiant form of thine;*
> *The veil of sense hangs dark between*
> *Thy blessed face and mine.*

How much easier if the 'veil of sense' were not there; if we had lived in His own day; accompanied Him in the days of His flesh! How wonderfully well we can understand the desire expressed by Jemima Luke:

> *I think, when I read that sweet story of old,*
> *When Jesus was here among men,*
> *How He called little children as lambs to His fold,*
> *I should like to have been with them then.*

Would it have been easier to have believed in Christ if we had lived in His own day? I wonder. Probably it was harder for people to believe in Him then. To do so was to go completely against the advice and example of the religious authorities. To acknowledge the stupendous claims of this wandering teacher was to submit to criticism and ridicule. To follow Christ is not easy today, but how much more difficult then! And yet there were those who followed Him. Why? Because they were convinced of the truth of His teaching. They were certain. Like Peter, they could say: "You have the words of eternal life. ... You are the Holy One of God." (John 6 vv.68,69).

Among the things that can give to our lives this certainty and assurance is the testimony of these early disciples. We have it recorded in the Scriptures. We have it in this very Gospel. Set down for us, as well as for Theophilus, we have the solid truth about the things of our faith. We can see how they found their faith, how they became certain, what it meant to them. We can see these disciples after the death of Jesus, perplexed, distracted, unsure, afraid. We can see the re-assurance that came to them with the knowledge of the resurrection. We can see them going forth in the certainty of their faith, their hearts filled with assurance. Their Master was alive! They carried that message with them. It carried them through opposition, suffering, persecution, death, to the building of His Church and to the spreading of His Gospel. We have the record of that - the testimony of the disciples - which can help us in our search for conviction and assurance.

Then, too, we have the testimony of the Church. Through the ages there have been dark chapters in the story of the Church. It's history has been vitiated by blindness, stupidity, dissention, narrowness, because of the weak and fallible men and women who have belonged to it. Yet in spite of its many weaknesses, the Church has contained through the centuries men and women who have been sure and certain of their faith. They have been tested and tried and have not been found wanting. They have been the inspiration of every human effort for the uplifting of mankind.

Canon Peter Green once declared that ninety per cent of all the philanthropic and social work which is being done is being done by those who are followers of Jesus Christ. Why? Because there is a driving force behind the Christian - the Church to which he belongs. In spite of all its failures, the Church has been through the centuries a living testimony to the truth of the religion of Jesus.

We have considered the testimony of the disciples and the testimony of the Church. There is one other testimony still - the testimony of personal experience.

Thousands upon thousands have known the reality of communion, fellowship and prayer. They have come to their

Master weary, and worn, and sad. They have heard Him say, "Be of good cheer", and they have gone back into life strengthened and confident. Wherever men have had this personal experience of fellowship with Christ they have no need of arguments - they know!

What an uproar was caused by the healing of the blind man! What arguments they used, those authorities who would have denied the miracle. Jesus was a sinner. He could not have healed the blind man. How they tried to brow-beat the man's parents and the man himself. But argument is of little use against experience. "One thing I do know. I was blind but now I see!" (John 9 v.25). No argument can alter that.

When Paul was enumerating the resurrection appearances of Christ, he used these words: "Last of all he appeared to me." (1 Corinthians 15 v.8). If we can say that of our own experience, last of all He was seen by me; blessed me; forgave me; comforted me; strengthened me; then we have the surest proof of the certainty of those things wherein we have been instructed.

Upon what shall we base our faith? The testimony of the disciples, the testimony of the Church, the testimony of our own personal experience. If this is ours, then we know in Whom we have believed.

Worrying? – Don't

"Don't try!" "Don't try!"

Like a refrain the words ran through my head as the result of reading, rather belatedly, one of the late John Hilton's published broadcast talks.

The talk was entitled, *"Is it coincidence?"* In it he discusses that 'sixth sense' which enables people to see into the future and to 'know' things they could not possibly know. By way of illustration he uses several personal experiences, among them, one concerning a game of chess.

To begin the game his opponent took a white pawn, fumbled with it for a while under the table, then brought out both fists for Hilton to decide in which the pawn was hidden. Feeling rather dreamy, and not caring much about the game, Hilton touched the right fist. The hand opened and there was the pawn. "I knew it was there," he said. "Did you," replied his opponent, "then perhaps you could do it a second time?" "I believe I could," was the answer. "All right," came the challenge, "Try." He tried. Twelve times the pawn was fumbled with under the table and twelve times Hilton touched the hand that held it. "Keep on," said the friend, "see how many times you can do it." But at that moment the certainty was gone. Although he tried again, he failed.

Was that just a run of luck, or was there really some sixth sense which enabled him to know with certainty where the pawn was? The above experience, coupled with others of like nature, inclined Hilton to believe that there are occasions when, as he puts it, we can see through a brick wall and foresee what will happen tomorrow. But we cannot do it deliberately.

"I still doubt," he says, "whether you can read what is in another person's mind by trying. I still doubt whether anyone can foresee what will happen tomorrow by trying. But I am prepared to believe that any or all of them can be done provided you're not trying."

Don't try or you'll fail. That was the burden of his talk.

This is certainly true in some spheres, as we may very well have proved for ourselves. Take memory, for instance. We try hard to remember something - a name perhaps. We have almost got it. It is there at "the back of our heads" or "on the tip of our tongue"; but it still eludes us. The harder we try the further it seems to recede. We give up in disgust and then, half an hour later, when we are not trying, we remember it.

The same thing happens when we are looking for something that we have mislaid. We know it is in the room somewhere, but we just can't put our hands on it; all our searching is in vain. Then, when we have given up, and cease trying, we find it - by accident, when looking for something else. There is certainly something to be said for not trying.

Yet is this not a dangerous doctrine? If we never tried, nothing would ever be achieved. What about those maxims of the "try, try, try again" sort? Surely the secret of success lies in resolution, in doggedness, in keeping on, keeping on. In trying.

This apparent conflict brings us to the crux of the matter. As the Preacher in Ecclesiastes might have said: "there is a time for trying and a time to cease from trying." The time to cease from trying is when your trying makes you restless, troubled and distressed; when it leads to anxiety and worry.

Perhaps that is what John Hilton meant.

It is certainly what Jesus of Nazareth meant when He summed up His teaching about food and drink and clothing with the words: "Do not worry about your life, what you will eat or drink." (Matthew 6 v.25). But we must! - and we do! Food, drink, clothing - these are among the essentials of life. How could we live if we did not try for these things? We spend most of our time doing it. There are, however, those who try so hard to gather together the essentials of living that they miss the glory of life itself. It becomes a burden, an anxiety; a thing of strain and stress.

It is amazing that people try so hard, even to the point of fretfulness and worry, when there are so many examples to show the foolishness of such a proceeding.

We find such a lesson taught in fiction, for the novelist knows the uselessness of trying too hard. In *"Sorrell and Son"* Warwick Deeping tells how Kit Sorrell and his friend Maurice Pentreath prepared for their Science Tripos. Sorrell had worked through the term but a few days before the examination he relaxed, spending time playing tennis and loafing on the river. At eleven o'clock on the night before the examination he entered Pentreath's rooms to find him still stewing away at his books. Anxious, nervous, his eyes blurred and sunken, restless, unsure of himself - it was no surprise that Pentreath's head was muzzy and that his memory played him tricks. As a result he obtained a 'third' while Sorrell secured a 'first'. He tried too hard!

Hugh Walpole teaches the same lesson in *"Rogue Herries"*. David, forty year old son of Francis Herries, longed to get married and settle down with a home and family of his own. Try as he would, however, he could not fall in love. He tried to make himself do so, but it was of no use. He even became engaged to Christina Paul, but there was no love in the contract. It only led to unhappiness and restlessness. Both were relieved when the engagement was broken. Afterwards he was more restless still and began to believe that love and marriage was not for him. Then, one night, being away from home and seeking accommodation at a wayside inn, he met by chance Sarah Denburn. Without trying, he found himself hopelessly in love.

Maurice Maeterlinck suggests that we can try too hard in our search for happiness. He pictures for us the children leaving home in their search for the Blue Bird. Up hill and down dale they travel; into the past and into the future they peer; all to no purpose. They catch glimpses of the Blue Bird, but it always eludes them. It is not until they give up trying and return home that they find it. The Blue Bird was there all the time.

These illustrations have been taken from the realms of fancy (howbeit there is beyond the fancy the writer's knowledge of life). Here is one from actual experience.

In his book, *"The Christ of the Indian Road"*, Dr. E. Stanley Jones confesses that when he first went to India he tried too hard. "I was trying," he says, "to hold a very long line. A line that stretched clear from Genesis to Revelation, on to Western Civilisation and on to the Western Christian Church. I found myself bobbing up and down that line - fighting behind Moses and David and Jesus and Paul and Western Civilisation and the Christian Church." I was worried.

It wasn't until the sheer storm and stress drove him to it that he realised he must take his stand at Christ. "I saw that the Gospel lies in the person of Jesus, that He Himself is the Good News, that my one task was to live and present Him." In refusing to try to do so much the anxiety and worry left him and he found vitality, simplicity and success.

I wanted to finish this article with an illustration that would sum up neatly and succinctly all I have been trying to say. It wasn't as easy as I had hoped. I thought again; I thought and thought as hard as I could. The more I thought the more baffled I became. My mind was becoming chaotic with my efforts when I pulled myself up. What was I getting so worried about? What right had I to mix medicine for others if I was not prepared to take it myself? "Leave it alone," I said to myself, "it will come." Sure enough, it did - like a flash. Perhaps the words "leave it alone" gave me the clue. There came to my mind the jingle that we all learned in our childhood days, the significance of which we probably never really grasped:

> *Little Bo-Peep has lost her sheep*
> *And doesn't know where to find them.*

What is she to do? Become anxious and worried? "Get into a flap" as our modern expression has it? Not at all.

> *Leave them alone, and they'll come home*
> *And bring their tails behind them.*

Worrying? - Don't!